NEVER GIVE A
SUCKER AN EVEN
BREAK

NEVER GIVE A SUCKER AN EVEN BREAK

Tricks and Bets You Can't Lose

by John Fisher

PANTHEON BOOKS, NEW YORK

For my nephew, James

First American Edition

Copyright © 1976 by John Fisher

All rights reserved under International and Pan-American Copyright Conventions. Published in the United States by Pantheon Books, a division of Random House, Inc., New York, and simultaneously in Canada by Random House of Canada Limited, Toronto. Originally published in Great Britain by Elm Tree Books/Hamish Hamilton Ltd., London.

Library of Congress Cataloging in Publication Data

Fisher, John, 1945-
  Never Give a Sucker an Even Break.

  1. Cardsharping. I. Title.
GV1247.F57 1976   795   76-50097
ISBN 0-394-73330-4

Manufactured in the United States of America

Dialogue from the following W. C. Fields films is quoted with the permission of Universal City Studios, Inc.:

Million Dollar Legs (1932)
International House (1933)
Tillie and Gus (1933)
The Old Fashioned Way (1934)
It's a Gift (1934)
You're Telling Me (1934)
Mississippi (1935)
The Man on the Flying Trapeze (1935)
Poppy (1936)
Big Broadcast of 1938 (1938)
You Can't Cheat an Honest Man (1939)
My Little Chickadee (1940)
The Bank Dick (1940)
Never Give a Sucker an Even Break (1941)

Contents

Introduction

Ever since Satan beguiled Adam and Eve with his apple trick, charlatans, knaves and confidence tricksters have flourished. None, however, could have been more brazen in his fraud than Meriton Latroon, the hero of an anonymous picaresque novel, *English Rogue*, who flourished in the mid-seventeenth century. Whenever his thirst needed slaking he would saunter into an inn, take a scrap of paper and jot down the following poem:

> I saw a peacock with a fiery tail
> I saw a blazing star that dropped down hail
> I saw a cloud begirt with ivy round
> I saw a sturdy oak creep on the ground
> I saw a pismire swallow up a whale
> I saw a brackish sea brim full of ale
> I saw a Venice-glass sixteen yards deep
> I saw a well full of men's tears that weep
> I saw men's eyes all on a flaming fire
> I saw a house big as the moon and higher
> I saw the sun all red even at midnight
> I saw the man that saw this dreadful sight

Upon completion, he would proceed to bet the price of a tankard that he had in fact set eyes upon these additional Wonders of the World. The bet made, the money collected, he would then, for the first time, recite the couplets, reading in the punctuation he had craftily omitted in writing. And no one now could dispute what he said: "I saw a peacock. With a fiery tail, I saw a blazing star. That dropped down hail, I saw a cloud. Begirt with ivy round, I saw a sturdy oak." He had no need to continue to convince his victim that all was lost and ensure that soon his own tankard would be as brim-full of ale as the Venice-glass in the doggerel itself.

Latroon is only one of a whole covey of cozeners who have, through the ages, capitalised upon the shortcomings of a general public so gullible that it is prepared to bet on almost anything. In recent times no one has turned this failing to greater personal advantage than the scandalous octogenarian Alvin Clarence Thomas, or "Titanic Thompson", to use his nickname. Last heard of alive and well and living in Grapevine, Texas, he has brought the art of cozenage to a degree of Machiavellian ingenuity worthy of the greatest spies, politicians, and stage illusionists. When he was only eleven he bet a stranger that the very stone he threw into a fishing hole would be retrieved by his dog after only one plunge into the water. The sucker agreed, provided that the stone be identifiable in some way. He watched as the young "Titanic" obliged by marking the pebble. What he did not see, however, were the countless other stones the boy had been marking painstakingly in a similar fashion for days before he pulled the ruse. Doubtless, somewhere in Arkansas, they still rest at the bottom of that pond. It would have been hard for *any* dog not to have retrieved a winning pebble.

As he grew up, so the delight to be gained from discomfiting financially those unwary enough to be bilked, informed his whole way of life. The lengths he would go to became legendary. It was nothing for him to pull up a road sign twenty miles outside a town and then re-position it five miles nearer. When he next drove that way with a likely victim he'd swear that it couldn't be twenty miles into town. The gambler would pick up the gauntlet, confident that the highways department was beyond reproach. Of course, his pockets were considerably lighter when they did reach their destination. Sly stage management of this kind behind the scenes of a bet once led him to tether eight white horses at random crossroads passed by the train connecting New York's Pennsylvania Station and the Jamaica racetrack. He then boarded the locomotive himself and subtly inveigled a whole crowd of major league horse betters into jeopardising their cash on the number of pure white steeds they would spot on their journey. Only Titanic dared "guess" high. Working for Titanic Thompson was a haughty boastfulness ingrained in his character which encouraged the most level-headed of men to attempt to outsmart him at his own game. But in trying to teach him a lesson, they were of course playing straight into his hands, flies to his spider in no uncertain way.

The braggadocio was a trait which he shared with the one name which overshadows all others in any rogues' gallery of petty fraud, the great W. C. Fields, whose philosophy gives this volume its title, a philosophy acquired during an adolescent apprenticeship when – if his biographers are to be believed – scarcely a day went by when he was not bilked by some unscrupulous manager, agent, or partner. How much he lived up to it in real life is still a matter of conjecture, possibly because people insist upon looking in the wrong places. Paranoiac at the thought of being taken for a sucker himself, he seldom gambled, and then only on pool and golf, where his own keen manipulative ability gave him a decided advantage and the element of chance was minimised as a result. But even if each round of golf was approached with the psychology of the shell-game operator, one would do better to look at his negotiations with the film companies whose vast corporate sums were as red rag to the bull of his instinct for survival. It gave him immense satisfaction to rail a studio for servicing him with a script which he would promptly dismiss as being full of holes, whereupon he would offer to straighten it out for 15,000 dollars. The rate which he could thus command for a couple of sentences scrawled upon the back of an envelope or a cryptic mark or two on the pages of the original, made him a veritable Picasso of the storyline. The ultimate con, of course, was that, whatever the script, he usually only said what he wanted to say anyway.

In the films themselves, however, there is no debate. For most people the most memorable moments are those which crystallise the image of Fields the charlatan, whether peering suspiciously from behind a fan of five aces, manipulating paper money as he deftly shortchanges the box-office queue, or making the little pea skedaddle invisibly from one walnut shell to another. It does not matter that his bluff would frequently be called. In images like these his whole demeanour spells out fakery in the way Astaire spells out class. And while enhanced by the background of carnival sideshow, sleazy saloon and seedy county fair, he never needed the geographical advantage. One recalls the moment he enlists ventriloquism as a confederate and sells a "talking dog" to yet another sucker. The deal completed, the hound looks at its new owner and, by courtesy of the Fields larynx, declares, "Just for that, I'll never talk again." Fields gets the last laugh as he scampers away from the scene of the transaction prophesying: "Stubborn little fellow, he probably means it, too."

The psychology that makes such ruses work in the first place is not far removed from that called into play by the professional magician. While W.C. would have abhorred the respectability such a label would have given his crafty shenanigans, and been apprehensive of the risk of exposure it courted, there is no doubt that with his flair for showmanship he would have made a great one. Bob Howard, his one time trainer and confidant, quoted by Robert Lewis Taylor, Fields's first and best biographer, once said: "When things were going smoothly, Bill was unhappy. He had to have somebody or something to pit his wits against." But the parallel with the likes of Harbin, Henning and Kaps suggested by that last sentence does not end there. As a juggler – he had, in his own words, a "fatal facility for juggling things" – he could beat the Chinese at their own game. But this went beyond his distrust of Orientals. Without question, he possessed the manipulative dexterity and poise needed in addition to the itch to deceive essential for all great hocus-pocus. So naturally did this come to him that once when he fell down stairs he did not spill one single drop of the martini in the glass in his hand at the time. Sprawled across the bottom step, he lifted it triumphantly: "Look! Not a drop spilled!" That he had broken the base of his spine faded into insignificance beside what was to him the highpoint of his juggling achievement.

One of the greatest and saddest ironies of his entire career is that at the height of his fame he refused an offer of $5000 a day from MGM to play the title role in *The Wizard of Oz*. The reason he gave was pressure of work in writing another film at the same time. One is tempted, however, to surmise that in no way was the patron saint of every knave who ever played upon the ignorance of those forever seeking the elusive pot of gold at the end of an imaginary rainbow, ever going to give substance to their dreams, even if for pot of gold it meant substituting the less desirable courage of a lion, heart of a tin man and brains of a scarecrow.

All of the gambits or "stings" in this book are in the spirit of Fields, most have long since been appropriated by the magical entertainer. As such they can still puzzle, infuriate and deceive, are still capable of winning a near-to-innocent drink at a bar. If the book has one purpose it is to entertain. Studied carefully, however, it can still educate one to the wiles and psychology of the major league swindlers and bunco-men. At the risk of sounding too much like those moralistic treatises by reformed gamblers that proliferated in the 1880s, not one person in the world is totally proof against the ingenuity of the most unscrupulous confidence-trickster. Perhaps none gave wiser advice than the gambler quoted by the hero of Damon Runyon's *Guys and Dolls*:

"Son, no matter how far you travel, or how smart you get, always remember this: someday, somewhere, a guy is going to come to you and show you a nice brand new deck of cards on which the seal is not yet broken, and this guy is going to offer to bet you that the Jack of Spades will jump out of this deck and squirt cider in your ear. But, son, do not bet this man, for as sure as you do, you are going to get an ear full of cider."

In short, never play another man's game or, if you must, make sure that you have done sufficient research to be capable of beating him on his own ground. The actor Thomas Mitchell had a favourite story which told of the visit he paid his friend born William Claude Dukenfield shortly before his death at the age of sixty-six on Christmas Day, 1946. Mitchell got the surprise of his life when he saw Fields, propped up in the sanatorium bed, out of all character thumbing through a copy of the Bible. "What are you doing?" Mitchell enquired. One can hear the reply that came from that velvety nasal drawl even now: "Looking for loopholes." Certainly, if anyone was going to find them, it was the comedy genius and magician-by-proxy whose spirit this book celebrates.

Drawing by Al Hirschfeld from the book *A Flask of Fields*.
©1972 Darien House Inc. All rights reserved.

Shameless Simplicity

In which the trickster challenges the victim to perform facile-sounding feats, both prosaic and bizarre, which prove themselves impossible upon the attempt.

Samson

"I can lick my weight in wildflowers."

Pick your prey and direct him to hold an ordinary wooden safety match between the fingers of one hand in such a way that it lies across the back of the middle finger, near the tip, and below the index and third fingers. The illustration shows the exact position. Emphasise that he must keep his fingers straight throughout, then challenge him to break the match.

However hard he presses upwards with the middle finger or downwards with the other two, he will amazingly not succeed. The reason is that the fingers lack certain muscles which we take for granted in other parts of the body, like the wrist, more conventionally used for breaking things.

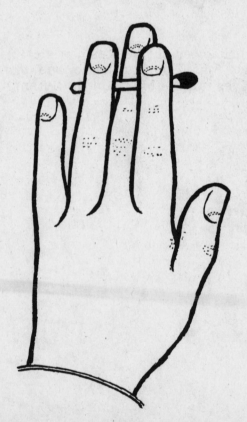

Should the challenge rebound on you, simply hold the match as shown, and keeping your arm and fingers straight, swiftly smack your hand down flat on the table top. That way you can break the match. With practice you can show off by breaking two or even three matches with this method all at the same time.

Molasses

"Molasses – the spreadingest stuff I ever saw in m'life."

Here is another seemingly simple proposition which will prove tantalising to anyone who attempts it without knowledge of the secret which makes it possible. Bet your victim that he cannot set light to a sugar cube with a match so that it burns with a flame. When he tries, he will produce only a brown treacly mess. Taking the cube from him, you ask him to light a match for you. When *you* apply it to the sugar, however, the cube bursts into flame.

What the sucker does not know is that the sugar catches fire only because you have managed, under the misdirection provided by his striking your match, to attach a very small quantity of cigarette ash to the cube. The ash – vegetable carbon – acts as a catalyst, the presence of which causes the sugar to catch fire. Provided that you do have an ashtray that is in use on hand when presenting the item, it is the work of a second to dip the sticky part of the cube into the ash for a small speck to adhere, thus winning the day for yourself once again.

Glacier

"Suffering sciatica – water!"

From hot cubes to cold ones! Present your dupe of the moment with an ice cube afloat in a glass of water and a short length of string; then wager that he will not be able to remove the ice cube from the glass with the string without tying any knots. He can try as much as he likes, but he will not succeed, not even by placing the string beneath the cube and attempting to balance it precariously.

When he finally gives in, take the string, soak it in the water, and then double it into a loop at the centre. Place the loop onto the ice cube and pour salt over them both. Wait a while and you will then be able to lift the ice cube with the string which will have become frozen to it. What actually happens is that the salt causes the ice to melt. Stop pouring the salt, however, and the water that results on the top of the cube will refreeze, but this time with the string embedded in it.

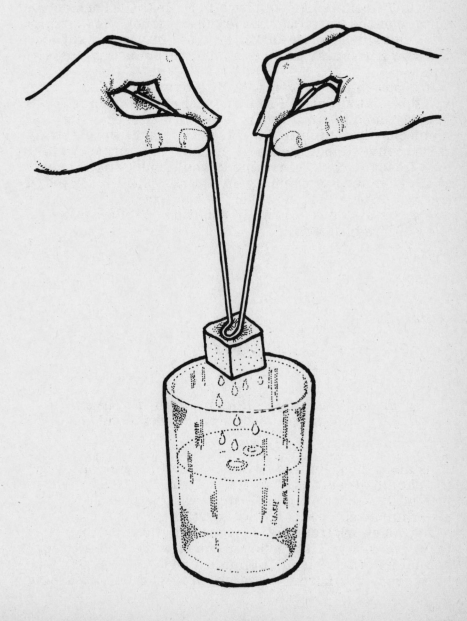

Meniscus

"My best friend died of drinking too much water. His was a case of internal drowning."

You show a glass of water, full almost to the brim, and a cork. You challenge your victim to float the cork on the surface of the water *without* letting it touch the glass. He tries, but whenever he thinks he is on the verge of success, the cork inexorably drifts to one side to bounce against the rim.

It is possible, however, to fulfil your conditions, even if you do cheat slightly. From another glass continue to fill the original one carefully until the surface of the water – or meniscus – is as high as possible without spilling, literally raised convex-fashion a fraction above the rim of the glass. Now float the cork. This time it would move to the centre of its own accord, even if you did not place it there. Of greater importance, however, is the fact that once it is there, it stays there, drawn irresistibly to the point where the water is highest.

Tipsy

On discovering his hip-flask unstoppered on its side:
"Somebody left the cork out of my lunch."

This mock-juggling ruse would have gladdened the heart (or should it be nose?), of the great W.C., whose own instinctive sense of equilibrium was, as we have seen, never impaired by alcoholic uncertainty.

Take the cork from the previous swindle and offer to pay for the next round if the victim can balance it edge to edge on the rim of a bottle full of liquid, and then using only one hand pour a drink from the same bottle without disturbing the balance of the cork. He would have to be a skilled juggler merely to balance the cork in the first place, let alone to embellish the feat by pouring a glass.

The secret is pretty sneaky. Take two forks and stick them into the cork as shown, the prongs almost interlocking. Just ensure, if the cork is not straight-sided, that the handles point downwards away from the wider end of the cork which should be at the top of the arrangement. The cork should now balance quite easily on the rim of the bottle for the scientific reason that the addition of the cutlery shifts the centre of gravity of the entire structure directly below the actual point of balance. Pouring from the bottle will alter the angle of the bottle itself, but will not disturb the cork which will remain perpendicular, as long as you pour from the side of the rim opposite to the point of balance. You will not be able to empty the bottle, but you should be able to pour at least half of the contents without spoiling your success.

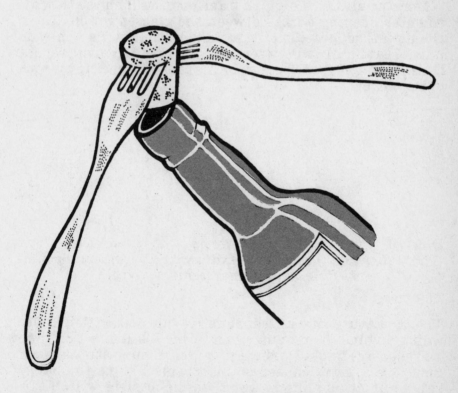

Obviously, practise with caution the first few times. You will soon develop an uncanny knack for handling the props and find that the challenge almost works itself for you.

Mixture

W.C.:   *Bring me a drink.*
Waiter: *Water, sir?*
W.C.:   *A little on the side – very little.*

Still at the bar, find two small jigger glasses, one of which you fill to the brim with whisky, the other with water. Take a visiting card or playing card and place it over the mouth of the glass of water, carefully inverting this and placing both card and glass on top of the glass of whisky. Make sure that the rim of the top glass is in exact alignment with that of the lower. Challenge someone that you can now make the water and whisky change places without altering the positions of the glasses in any way.

Merely pull out the card a fraction of an inch to allow air to enter, leaving a gap between the glasses which allows the liquids supposedly to mix. In fact, that is what they do not do. Gradually the water and whisky will transpose, not through magic, but because of the greater specific gravity of the water.

Cocktail

On awakening to find a full-grown goat in bed beside him: "Right then and there I swore that I would never again poison my system with a maraschino cherry."

The literature of baffledom is overloaded with puzzles which involve the moving of matches. While most of them have become hackneyed over the years, such stunts, ideal for the bar, have caused so many small sums to change hands that this volume would be incomplete without at least one. Moreover, it was not difficult to decide which variation on the theme would have held most attraction for Fields.

20

Place four matches to form a Martini glass as shown, adding a small coin to denote a cherry. The object is to move two matches in such a way that the cherry will end up outside the glass. You must not move the cherry. The glass must stay the same shape.

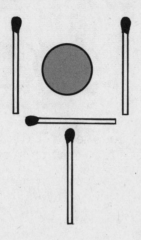

You can, if you wish, mislead the victim upon whom you spring the puzzle by suggesting some solutions that don't quite fit. You could, for example, move matches C and D but that would only turn the glass upside down and technically the cherry would still be inside.

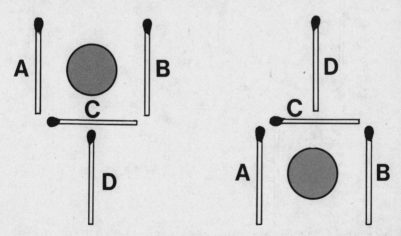

Alternatively, you could make the adjustments depicted in the next illustration, thus achieving your end, but having to move *three* matches, C, D, and A, to do so.

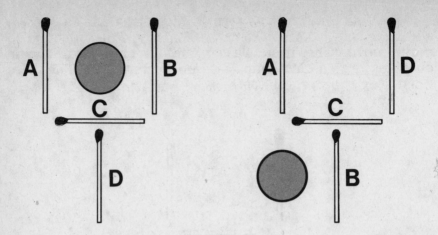

The actual solution does technically require two moves; the catch resides in the fact that they could be interpreted as one and a half.

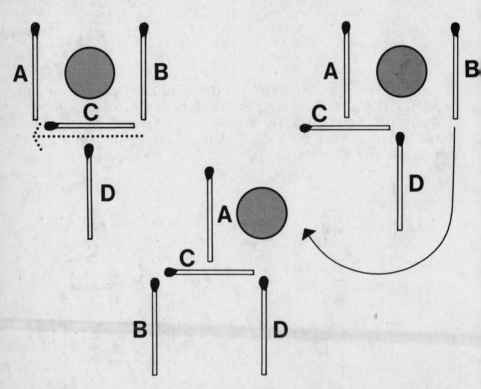

First slide C half-way along to the left. Then bring B down to the end of C, as shown. Now the cherry should be out on its own, the way, no doubt, Fields would have wished!

Exchequer

Disgruntled Man: You're a fraud, a charlatan, and a rogue. sir!
W.C.: Ahhh – is that in my favour?

For originality and effect this occupies the same high position in the hierarchy of coin-sliding problems as the last item holds in the realm of match-moving. You have to arrange ten copper and ten silver coins alternately in four rows of five coins, as shown. The coins should be as near equal in size as possible. British five pence and two pence pieces are ideal.

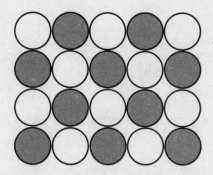

The wager is to arrange the coins into segregated horizontal rows of copper and silver coins. But there is one condition: you can touch only two coins. That's all you say. In actual fact, while you may touch only two, there is nothing to stop you moving more. Extend your right index and second fingers and put them on coins A and B respectively.

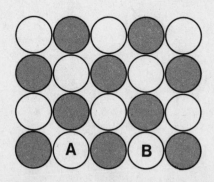

Then, sliding both coins against the table surface, swing them up and around until they occupy these positions:

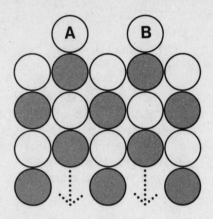

Then slide them down in the direction of the arrows, each one pushing three coins ahead of it. The coins should then arrive in the stipulated position.

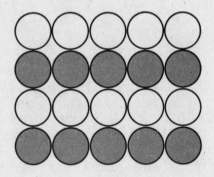

Pick-up

"Me dishonest? Meishack, Shadrack and Abednego!"

You arrange nine coins in three rows of three to make a square. You contribute five or more of the coins yourself; the rest must be contributed by your innocent gull. You then offer him a chance of pocketing both yours and his if he can pick up all nine coins in four continuous straight lines. There is only one stipulation. Each line must start at the end of the previous one. Should he fail, you pocket the coins.

Try as he may, it is not possible to gather the nine in anything less than five lines, *unless* he knows the secret stratagem. The catch is in the wording, which says nothing about extending imaginary lines beyond the coins. The sucker will assume – wrongly – that each line must end on a coin. This is how you prove him wrong:

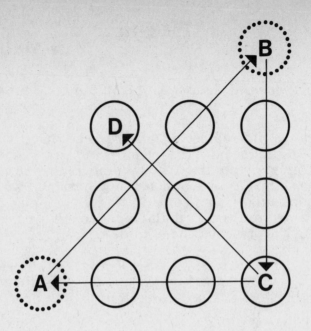

Pick up the three coins in the bottom row in the direction of the arrow, counting "one" as you arrive at A. Proceed from A as shown, picking up the intervening coins and counting "two" as you reach B. Then bend south, picking up the two coins remaining on the right-hand side, and coming to rest, "three", at C. Finally, complete the operation on the final diagonal, ending with "four" at D. And don't forget to pocket the coins.

Hazard

"A man who over-indulges lives in a dream. He becomes conceited. He thinks the whole world revolves around him – and it usually does."

Equip yourself, if possible, with a dice cup or failing that a straight-sided tumbler. Hold the cup, as shown, with a die – a lump of sugar would do – between thumb and forefinger. Balance a second die on top of the first. The challenge is to toss the first die up into the cup, and then to repeat the process with the second, ending with two dice in the cup. It sounds easy, until one tries.

Most people have no difficulty catching the first die, but as soon as they set the second on its upward course, the first flies out. There is a secret, of course. Instead of tossing the second die up into the air like the first one, you hold your hand high, release the die and then suddenly lower the cup to catch it on the downward swing. Don't descend too fast or else the first die will fly out again; just fast enough so that the cup comes beneath the falling die before it reaches the floor.

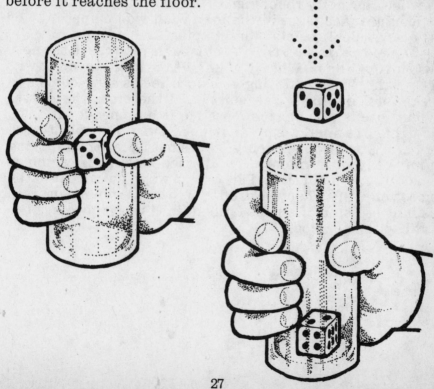

Untouchable

W.C.: *Was I in here last night and did I spend a twenty dollar bill?*
Barman: *Yeh!*
W.C.: *Oh, boy! What a load that is off my mind! I thought I'd lost it.*

The sucker will really think you are out of your mind on this one. You display a crisp, unwrinkled treasury note or bill and explain that when you drop it, his task is to catch it before it falls to the floor. If he succeeds he can pocket the note; if he fails he must pay you ten pence for the attempt. You demonstrate on yourself and it all appears so simple, but whenever the sucker tries, he will be attempting the impossible.

The secret is all a matter of fingers and thumbs. You must hold the note between the finger and thumb at one end, the length of the note pointing downwards; your victim must position his own finger and thumb on either side of the note at the centre, as close as he can get to the paper without actually touching it. In fact you give him every opportunity to place his hand in what would appear to be the most ideal position for grasping it.

Explain again that the object is for him to catch the note when you drop it. When you do release it, however, it will slip right through his fingers before he has had a chance to register his senses. The newer and therefore the flatter your note is, the more impossible it becomes for it to be caught. Just make sure that each time you release the money, you do so suddenly, as a surprise, without giving him the briefest moment of advance warning in which to anticipate your actions. The reason why you can catch the note yourself – when you drop it – is because your own brain is in possession of all the facts needed to synchronise the grab with the release.

Never Play Cards with Strangers

In which the charlatan is introduced to the peculiar properties of the pasteboards when entrusted to digits as dextrous and devious as his own.

Second-deal

*To Mae West: Do you play cards? I'll show you a few card
tricks. Show you the first one or two for
nothing. Then if you wish to make a wager. . . .*

S. W. Erdnase, author of *The Expert at the Card Table*, the
classic work on gambling technique with playing cards,
wrote: "To become an adept at second dealing is as
difficult a task as can be given in card handling, but once
acquired, like many other arts, it is as easy as habit." If
you wish to master this most impressive of sleights,
Erdnase's book is where you should look first. If, though,
you lack the patience to persist with the genuine gambit
until it becomes a habit, the following will prove an
admirable routine for simulating the function of the
sleight, without at all detracting from the stunned look on
the face of the onlooker.

Before the demonstration you will need to make a secret
arrangement of cards at the top of the pack. Working face-
down from the top place any three jacks, then an indifferent card, then the fourth jack. Begin by casually
false shuffling and/or cutting the cards. (See the Appendix
for simple methods.) Explain briefly what a second or even
third deal is supposed to achieve, namely the secret
retention of respectively one or two cards on top of the
deck as the card beneath is dealt onto the table. Deal out
two hands of three cards to the sucker and yourself. When
you deal the sixth card, don't place it down; merely use it
to scoop up your other two cards and place all three face-
down on top of the pack. Turn over the spectator's hand. It
reveals three jacks.

You now explain that by putting those cards back on top
of the pack, you can, through using the second and third
deals, immediately deal three jacks into that same hand
again. Put them back on top of the pack and again deal two
hands, scooping yours back again to the top of the pack
with the sixth card. Again, turn over the spectator's cards.
Again, he gets three jacks. Provided that you deal and pick
up the cards at a steady momentum, no one should notice
that one of the jacks has changed its suit. It will be
assumed that they are the same three cards. At no point, of
course, mention the suits of the jacks. As long as you
always scoop your hand back as described, thus reinstat-

ing the original set-up, you can carry on the demonstration virtually *ad infinitum*. However, three or four times is about enough. Don't go on so long that people begin to suspect that your "recoil" of the top card is not so much "invisible" as non-existent!

Casework

W.C.:   *Would you like to engage in a little game of cut – high card wins?*
Gambler: *What stakes?*
W.C.:   *Make it easy on yourself.*
Gambler: *A hundred dollars, gold.*
W.C.:   *I'll cover that. I'm travelling a little light. The country is fraught with marauders. I'll give you my personal IOU, a thing I seldom give to strangers.*

The ability to memorise cards in and out of sequence is an important weapon in the armoury of the card-sharper. Obviously if one can remember which cards have been played and exposed during the course of a game, one will have an edge over the opponent who just lets them pass by. The technical term here is "casing the deck". The following demonstration, while requiring some memory work of the very simplest order, could win for you the reputation of having developed this ability to super-human dimensions.

Have someone shuffle the pack. Take it and spread the cards face-up on the table. Mention the gambler's ability to memorise the order of complete packs, while you survey the cards as if you were doing just that. In fact, you only remember the top card, say the seven of hearts. Gather the pack and place it face-down on the table. Ask the victim to cut off a packet of cards and place them away from you. Now issue your challenge; namely that by looking at the top card of one heap, you can always assess the card at the top of the other. Openly peek at the value of the top card of the nearer (originally bottom) half, (say the two of clubs), and without showing it replace it saying, "The card on this pile tells me that the card on the far pile

31

is the seven of hearts." He turns it over. It is! Complete the cut, (thus putting the two of clubs at the top of the pack), and have someone cut the cards again. Once more you look at the top card of the bottom pile, replace it and state your case, "The card on this pile tells me that the card on the far pile is the two of clubs."

And so it goes on indefinitely. You're getting all the information you need for the divination right under their noses, but the sheer audacity of the system provides its own misdirection. If anything, you'll be accused of using a marked deck! And that's another story.

Aces

W.C.:   *Don't show it to me. The cards are a gentleman's game. I don't want to look at it.*
Gambler: *(cutting to a card) King!*
W.C.:   *Oh! (Then cutting his card – a two!) Ace!*
Gambler: *I didn't see it!*
W.C.:   *(Fumbling through the pack) Well, well, here you are – here you are, Nosy Parker – ace! I hope that satisfies your morbid curiosity.*

Another legendary demonstration of the card-sharper's expertise is his ability to cut instinctively to the four aces in a shuffled pack. When practised by the high-powered gambler it most probably entails sheer twenty-four carat skill. Alternatively, it could be a simple exercise in hanky-panky like the one that follows.

The feat will naturally be more impressive with a borrowed pack, which you will have to gimmick in a surprising fashion. Politely take your leave of whatever company you are in and pay a supposedly natural visit to the bathroom. No one must know at this point that in your pocket is a pack, the newer the better, which you have secretly waylaid from your host. You need one other thing, a pair of nail-clippers, which you should carry with you. Lock the door behind you and get to work. Take the aces and with the clippers trim a slight crescent from each of their top right and lower left face-up corners. Make the cuts clean and round, and then shuffle the cards back into the pack. If when you now riffle the outer left edge of the face-down pack, you cannot instantly detect the cards, it will be necessary to make the cuts deeper.

Later when you come to demonstrate your skills, produce the pack as one provided by your host. Run through it and take out the four aces. Hand the rest of the pack out for shuffling, then ask the person holding the pack to take any ace and to lose it in the pack. The three other aces are each lost in a similar fashion. Finally the cards are handed back to you. It is now a simple matter merely to riffle the outer left corner of the face-down pack and cut at the desired cards. A slight break in the action will automatically identify an ace for you. Repeat with the other three aces as dramatically as possible while still retaining some vestige of credibility!

If you wish to make the experiment appear even more impressive, you could trim the red and black aces in opposing corners, as shown in the illustration. You would then have no difficulty in cutting to the aces in the order of colours called out by the spectator.

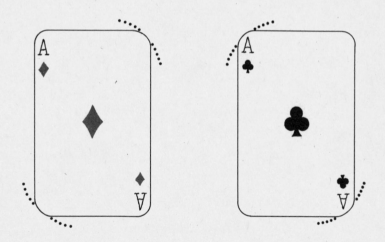

Circus

"Never give a sucker an even break. Why? Most people have a feeling they are going to be reincarnated and come back to this life. Not me. I know I'm going through here only once."

The following swindle has long been known affectionately as the Circus card trick, in recognition of the frequency with which it once appeared alongside the walnut shells and "find-the-lady" in the repertoires of mountebanks who attached themselves to circuses on tour.

Offer the pack for shuffling. Take it back, fan the cards, and have one chosen and noted. While the victim shows his card to the other people in the audience, you are stealthily remembering the card at the bottom of the pack in your hands. This will be your key card. Have the chosen card replaced on top and the cards cut several times, making sure that his card is lost somewhere in the centre of the pack.

Taking the cards yourself you now announce that you will – surprise, surprise – attempt to find his chosen card. You deal the cards singly from the top of the face-down pack into a face-up pile. Keep dealing until you come to your key card. The next card dealt will be the selected one, the identity of which you must remember. Then deal four or five cards more. Take the next card, hesitate and deal it face-down separately onto the table. Now bet the victim that the next card you turn over will be his chosen card. He will have noticed that you missed his card about half-a-dozen ago and will gladly accept the bet, whereupon you do not turn over the face-down card, but go back to the face-up pile, find his card, and turn that over *face-down!*

Shill

W.C.: *During the night, I was awakened. A thief had broken*
into my tent and tried to roll me for my poke.
Son: *Roll you for your poke – what kind of talk is that?*
W.C.: *He tried to steal my pocketbook, son.*

So far I have deliberately avoided swindles which depend
for their chicanery on the use of a confederate or "shill",
the technical term applied in gambling circles to the
employee of the sideshow or gambling house who bets his
master's money under pretence of being a legitimate
player in order to stimulate extra business. In the following, however, a shill is used in a special way. You can, of
course, appoint him in secret beforehand and divide the
profits between yourselves afterwards. What sets the game
apart, however, is that you can also present it as a
demonstration, openly nominating a spectator to play the
part of the shill. While he'll find himself winning some of
the time, he will still end up as puzzled as the sucker
himself as to why the sucker should lose *all* of the time.

Discard the jokers from the pack beforehand and arrange
the rest of the cards so that the colours are alternated
throughout, namely red, black, red, black, and so on. In the
performance you cut the cards into two halves ensuring
that the bottom card of one half is red, of the other half
black. Now riffle shuffle these halves together. If you can
trust his proficiency with the deck, you can even allow the
sucker to do this for you. He may also cut the cards a few
times as long as he completes the cut each time. Take the
pack from him and deal the cards into four face-down piles
of thirteen cards each.

So far everything must appear transparently fair, but
what neither sucker nor shill will be aware of is the curious
relationship that exists between the first two piles dealt
(we'll call them A and B) and again between the second two
piles (C and D). For every red card in pile A, the card in the
corresponding position in B will be black. Similarly, for
every black card in A, the corresponding card in B will be
red. The same applies to C and D. Deal the cards simultaneously from the tops of two related piles, and you'll deal
red and black pairs each time. None of this you reveal to
the audience.

The sucker is now invited to take a pile. If he chooses A you discard B or vice versa. Then nominate another spectator as your shill and let him take one of the remaining heaps, C or D. You take the last heap. Another example: if the sucker chooses D, C would be discarded, and the shill and yourself would be left with A and B.

At last we come to the object of the game! The three of you are to deal face-up one at a time, together, cards from the top of your pile. Each time the party with the odd-coloured card wins. Thus, if two people turn up red cards, and one a black, the one with the black wins. If you all turn up the same colour (which you can't) then it's a draw. You now proceed with the turning. Not once in his whole sequence of thirteen cards will the sucker win! The reason is easy to deduce. The shill and yourself will always deal a red-black pair between you because you have specially related piles. This means that whenever the sucker deals a red, whichever of you has a black *must* win. Likewise, whenever he deals a black, the one with the red *must* win. The sucker must lose every time. He may even shuffle his cards before he deals, but in no way can he deal a winning card. Think about it. It works!

Kentucky

"Don't forget – Lady Godiva put everything she had on a horse."

If you discard from a full pack of fifty-two cards one heart, one club and one spade, and then deal the remaining forty-nine cards into four piles determined by their suits, you will find, upon exhausting the pack, that one pile, namely the diamond one, will contain one card more than the other piles. That should be obvious. In the early fifties, however, a magician called Tony Koynini, flagrantly defying the obvious, used this knowledge as the basis of a simulated horse-race game in which the operator wins every time. His routine, entitled "Derby", was full of subtleties – enough to throw anyone familiar with the basic principle off the scent – which it would be unethical to disclose here. The following, however, presents the basic bones of the game in simplified form.

In addition to a pack of cards, you will also need sixteen matches and some coins. The matches are arranged in two parallel lines and represent sections of the track along which the horses, the four aces, will race. A move of an ace/horse is determined by dealing a card of the corresponding suit from the top of the pack. Thus the idea of numbers of cards in a pile is subtly translated into one of moves along a track. If the cards of one suit outnumber those of the other three, it can be contrived that the ace/horse of that suit will reach the finishing line, as represented by the last match, first.

Since you are not going to exhaust a full pack of forty-nine cards (i.e. fifty-two minus three), you will need to stack the cards first. Make a pile containing in any order any six hearts, six clubs, six diamonds and six spades, but excluding the four aces. Place these cards face-down on top of the remaining cards. Then insert the four aces throughout the bottom half of the pack, ensuring that each face-down ace is above a card of a matching suit. This is all the preparation needed.

When ready to play bring out the pack and have your three opponents each nominate an ace/horse for themselves in turn. As they call them out, you remove them in turn from the face-up pack placing each card as shown at the starting post. You emphasise their absolutely free choice in this respect and that they have left you – without any choice – with the fourth ace. With the cards facing you, fan through them and remove this last ace, say the ace of clubs. In doing so, however, you have to add to the top of the pack an additional card of that suit (here a club) from the bottom part of the deck. This is facilitated by the fact that because of the set-up immediately below the ace as it faces you is just such a card. As you fan through, push the two cards into alignment, and casually break the pack above the ace, taking the ace itself and all the cards beneath it away in the right hand. Then transfer the double card to the back of the pack, immediately returning the rest of the cards in the right hand to the face of the deck. Square up the cards in the hands, and flip the pack over face-down in the left hand, whereupon you deal the ace face-up into the starting position left nearest you.

The situation is now that amongst the top twenty-five cards of the face-down pack, the clubs outnumber the other suits by one card. You could if you wished start playing immediately. It is better, though, to have the cards shuffled at this point. Either false shuffle (see Appendix), or, more impressively, thumb off the top twenty-five cards to one contestant, and divide the rest of the pack between the other two. A slight pencil dot in the top left and bottom right-hand corner of the twenty-fifth or twenty-sixth card will enable you to fan off the correct number without counting. Just make sure that you gather the cards back in the proper order, namely with the larger packet of twenty-five on top. False cut (again, see Appendix), and hand the cards to another party ready for dealing, not however until you have all placed your bets on your ace/horse. The idea is that whoever wins, collects all.

Now the dealing begins. Whenever a spade is dealt from the top of the pack, the ace of spades moves forward one space as marked by a match. Likewise, the other cards. You will *always* reach the finishing line first in spite of what must appear the most impossible conditions.

Jonah

"Boys, this mummy sitting over here inveigled me into a game of chance entitled . . . draw poker. I figured right from the start I'd have to shoot him. It was all I could do to take his money!"

This could be the most astonishing poker challenge of them all. When presented well, it appears as if the operator has absolutely no control over the cards, that the outcome of events is entirely in the hands of the sucker himself. This is as far removed from the truth as Fields himself was from taking holy orders.

Remove from the pack three sets of three of a kind plus one indifferent card, say three aces, three kings, three queens and a jack. The jack is the "Jonah" card, and the secret upon which your prosperity depends. However the cards are dealt between you and your victim, you will always win, provided that the odd Jonah card ends up in *his* hand.

There are several ways of ensuring that this happens. Have the three trios on the top of the face-down pack, the Jonah in the tenth position. Casually thumb off in batches the top nine cards, without counting them out loud. Hand them to the victim for shuffling. Let him now replace them on the pack and deal two hands of five cards. He'll get the Jonah!

If the Jonah card is secretly marked on its back – with gradual use all cards acquire identifying marks, nicks and scratches of some kind – you can play draw poker. Have him shuffle the ten cards and spread them face-down on the table. Both players must now draw cards alternately until each has a hand of five. Just make sure you don't pick up the Jonah card. If you draw first, there is no way he can avoid getting it; if he hasn't taken it beforehand, just make sure that it's the last card he picks up. If he draws first, the odds are still highly in your favour that the Jonah will not be the last card on the table, the only card you *would have* to take. Should this happen, what is one small loss amonst so many gains?

For another variation, have him shuffle and cut the ten. Take them back and fan them slightly, noting whether the Jonah is at an odd or even position from the top. If odd, deal two hands yourself. If even, stress that he did all the mixing himself and hand them back for him to deal. You haven't done anything to the cards except touch them, so he should have no suspicions. Still he gets the Jonah.

Finally, assemble the ten cards with the Jonah at the top. Shuffle the packet, keeping it at the top if you can do so casually and convincingly. Start to deal, the Jonah to the sucker, the next to yourself, then pause as if having a bright idea. To make it even fairer for the victim you will show him the cards as they are dealt, stud poker fashion, and he can keep or reject them accordingly. Whichever four he chooses to complete his hand, it is a foregone conclusion that he is going to lose anyhow.

If you doubt the invincibility of the hand without the Jonah, consider this. Should the sucker get a pair (say two aces), you will beat him with two pairs (two queens and two kings). Should he get two pairs (say two aces and two kings), you'll beat him with three of a kind (three queens). Should he get three of a kind (say, three kings), you'll amaze him with three of a kind (say, three queens), *and* a pair (two aces), thus making a full house!

Martini

"Shades of Bacchus!"

If any gaffed deal ought to have appealed to the great W.C. it was this one, admirably suited as it is to being performed in what passes as a typically Fieldsian alcoholic haze.

You will need a pack with a one-way backs design, the term used to describe cards with backs so designed that some distinguishing mark will differentiate one end of a card from the other. Pictorial backs lend themselves most easily to the idea. Imagine a pack with a dog motif, not that Fields could! Place the cards all the same way with the picture right way up. Have one chosen, secretly reverse the pack end for end, and then offer the pack for the return of the card. If you now look at the backs of the cards you can instantly detect the chosen card. It's the one that is upside-down.

Ideally borrow such a pack and secretly set all the backs one way with the exception of the spades, which go in the opposite direction. You can now demonstrate how Fields would have dealt the cards in one of his more inebriated moments. Shuffle the cards as impressively as you can, making sure that you do not disturb the end for end arrangement. Act the part of the supposedly befuddled charlatan as well as you can, and deal cards haphazardly – in no regular rotation to north, east, south or west – into four hands in any sequence. At least that is how it appears. In actual fact, you contrive to deal the thirteen cards with reversed backs into your own hand and to make sure that each other hand also gets thirteen. Everyone turns over their cards and, such are the powers of alcohol, it's the drunk who gets the grand slam!

Automatic

On being coerced into playing a game:
W.C.:   Poker? Is that the game where one receives five cards? And if there's two alike that's pretty good, but if there's three alike, that's much better?
Gambler: Oh, you'll learn the game in no time.

Most audiences will be as aware of the device of stacking cards in a pre-arranged sequence whereby they will arrive in the right hands as they are of marked cards and second-dealing. Here, however, you allow the *spectators* to arrange the cards in the sequence *they* desire and prove that beyond all the odds the cards will come out as *you* want them to.

First take the twenty high cards from the pack, the aces, kings, queens, jacks and tens. The spectators nominate amongst themselves three of their number to play. They are each asked in turn to suggest a combination of five cards from the twenty, disregarding the suits at this stage. As the various hands are called, you lay them face-up on the table in front of the person who called them, placing the last five in front of yourself. Your only stipulation is that they should not call high hands. All this enables you to build up the hand you eventually want to receive as you are setting the cards down. Suppose you want a royal flush in spades. In arranging the hands, just make sure that in one hand a spade goes second, in another third, in another fourth, and in the last both first and last. An example layout is shown in the illustration. When you pick up the hands, first take the one with two spades (B), place it face-up on the hand with the spade second (A), place both on the hand with the spade third (C), and finally drop them all on the remaining hand (D).

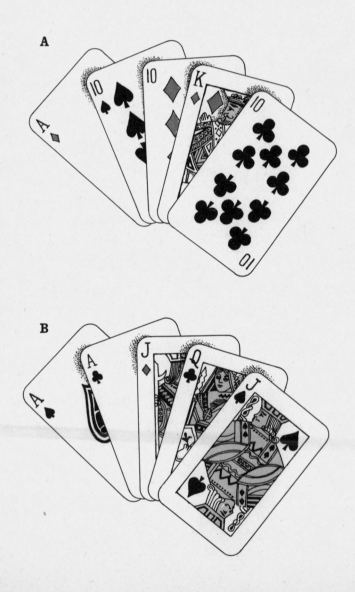

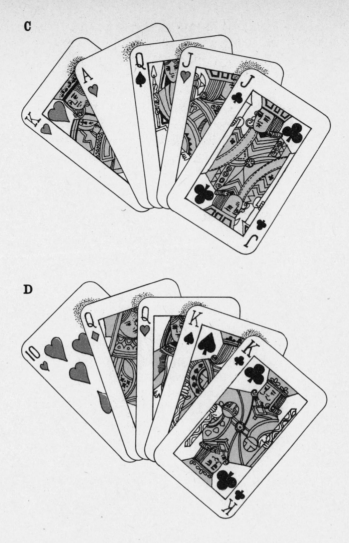

Turn the twenty cards face down and you will have a spade at every fourth card in the pile. False shuffle (for which see the Appendix), if you wish; then keep cutting the packet until a spade appears on the bottom. Deal four hands of five cards and you'll get a royal flush in spades!

Honesty

"Now listen you, gentlemen of the jury. In this game I deal myself four aces, all regular. What is my astonishment when High-Card there lays down five aces, against my four? I'm a broad-minded man, gents. I don't object to nine aces in one deck, but when a man lays down five aces in one hand – ! And besides, I know what I dealt him!"

In the last dodge the cards were set up brazenly under the very noses of the spectators without their being aware of what was happening. Here you rely on a set-up, but leave it to the manufacturer of the playing cards to do the hocus-pocus for you.

Many brands of cards come from the factory with each suit arranged in order from ace through to king. Locate such a source of cards and you'll be able to give the following demonstration of how a crooked gambler works and how honesty always (?) wins! Read the following through with an appropriately set-up pack in hand and you will see that it practically works itself.

Begin by stressing that you use a new pack. Break the seal, and without disturbing the order of the rest of the cards, remove the jokers and any advertising or score cards. Have the cards cut several times, making sure that you end up with a 6, 7, 8, 9, 10, jack, queen, king or ace on the bottom of the pack. Deal seven cards face-down from the top, one to each of seven poker players. Then explain how crooked gamblers often resort to a bottom deal, a device for dealing the card they want from the bottom of the pack, yet making it appear as if it were coming from the top. Show what you mean. Deal the first six cards of the next round to their respective hands, then clumsily take the bottom card and deal it to your hand. Deal seven more cards from the top, making three in each hand, and then repeat the obvious bottom-deal to yourself fourth time around. The fifth card for each hand is then dealt conventionally from the top of the pack.

Now you explain how dishonesty never wins. Turn over each of the six hands in turn and reveal that *each* contains a full house, namely three of a kind and a pair! Then reveal your crooked hand. All you have is three of a kind. You would have lost even by cheating. Had you been really honest, you state, you would have discarded the crooked hand and dealt yourself another five off the top of the pack. This you proceed to do. Turn over your new hand slowly. It will be a straight flush, five cards of the same suit in correct sequence, far superior to any full house.

Getaway

Judge: Have you anything more to say before I find you guilty?
W.C.:   So you're going to deal from a cold deck, eh?

To close this section on a note of dubious hilarity, bet a poker player that he can't beat four aces with a royal straight flush. He will accept enthusiastically, all the while puzzling over where he can lay his hands on the nearest copy of Hoyle or Scarne, from which to quote the rules and prove you wrong. Before he gets there, however, you take the pack, remove your four of a kind and nonchalantly pass him the rest of the cards with the line, "There's my four aces. Where's your royal straight flush?" At which point you run.

Follow Me —
If You Can!

In which the trickster unblushingly inveigles the unsuspecting gull into following the leader – but in less innocent a fashion than that exercised in infancy.

Edifice

On standing for the Presidency: "It is of interest to note that I have remained true to the hobby of crap-shooting ever since, and on this I rely for a great many votes."

The basic challenge presented here is best summed up by the illustration. You have three straight dice, similar in every respect and ideally about three-quarters of an inch square. Take two of them and wager anyone that he cannot balance them successfully side by side on top of the third at an angle as shown. It's impossible, unless you happen to know the *modus operandi*.

While the dice are falling about all over the place from the sucker's frustrated attempts, discreetly apply a slight amount of saliva to the tip of your right index finger. Transfer the moisture to the "one-spot" side of one of the dice, at the same time as the left hand picks up another die. Bring them together, the two "one-spots" face to face. A gentle squeeze and the dice will adhere as a single unit, making the balancing possible in the process. As you take the two dice down again, separate them between your fingers, remembering to rub off any tell-tale moisture before handing them over to yet another victim to try his luck.

Pyramid

"I'll knock 'em for a row of lib-labs."

This sting would have appealed to Fields the juggler, Fields the pool hustler, and Fields the carnival knave at one and the same time. You take three pool or billiard balls and place them on the table to form a triangle, each ball touching the other two. You then take a fourth ball and carefully rest it on top of the triangle to form a pyramid. The pyramid stays erect. This you achieve time and time again, but each time the sucker attempts to duplicate your result, the balls in the triangle roll away before he can bring the fourth ball to rest.

Your secret gimmick could not be more obvious, namely the chalk. If it is green, draw a line with it around the green ball about one third up, connecting in fact three imaginary points on its circumference where it will make contact with the triangular base of the pyramid. If the chalk is white, use a white ball. You form the triangle with any three other balls, then gently place the gimmicked ball on top, making sure that the chalked line is in position and holding the triangle with your free hand until you feel that the fourth ball has gripped. Carefully take your hands away and the pyramid should stand there.

Eventually dismantle the structure and in the process of taking off the top ball rub the chalk off on your hand. Now challenge the sucker to duplicate what you have done. As he is chasing balls all over the table in his attempt, you have ample opportunity to "chalk up" another ball in secret ready to perform the dodge again.

Tumbler

"I was in love with a beautiful blonde once – she drove me to drink – 'tis the one thing I'm indebted to her for."

Line up three tumblers in a row, designating the one at your extreme left 1, the one in the centre 2, the one at the extreme right 3. You can mark the positions with playing cards should you wish. Tumbler 2 is right way up, the two outside tumblers upside down. You now show how with three moves you can leave all three tumblers standing *mouth upward*, ready for filling. Each *move* must consist of turning two tumblers over at the same time, one tumbler in each hand.

You demonstrate, making it look absurdly simple. Merely turn:

1 Tumblers 2 and 3
2 Tumblers 1 and 3
3 Tumblers 2 and 3

chanting the positions as you do so. Emphasise the numerical sequence: " 2 and 3, 1 and 3, 2 and 3". Now you challenge the sucker to do the same, at which point you make the one sneaky move upon which your prosperity as a carnival pitchman depends. Nonchalantly turn tumbler 2 upside down. It all seems fair, the tumblers back as they started; but there is, in fact, a subtle difference. The centre glass is still standing the opposite way to the two end tumblers, but now it is mouth downward while the others are mouth upward. However religiously he follows through the "2 and 3, 1 and 3, 2 and 3" ritual, the sucker will not finish with three tumblers mouth upward. His tumblers have to end all mouth downward, ready for emptying!

The mathematics of his starting position are so loaded against him that it is impossible for him to end up with three tumblers right way up ready for filling, *however many* regulation moves he makes.

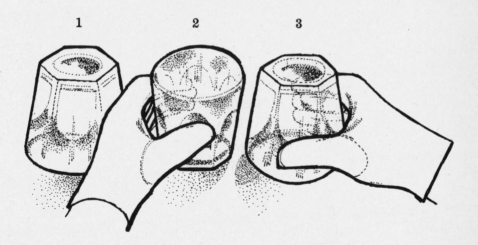

Transparent

"I may be a liar, but at least I'm a gentleman."

Remove the cellophane tube from a cigar and squeeze it flat by drawing it between the index and second fingers of one hand. At the centre point along one edge tear a minute notch with your thumbnail, and then halfway between this notch and the end of the tube make a second notch. If you have difficulty in making the notches you can get the same effect by pricking the cellophane wrapper with a pin in the appropriate places. This is all done in secret, the device which enables you to bet with certainty that the sucker will not be able to perform the simplest action with the cellophane, while you can.

Hold the cellophane in such a way that the notches face downwards, and tear the flattened tube into two. It should look as if you are tearing from the top, but you will find that with a downward move of one hand you can tear upwards at the centre notch. This is what you do, the fingers and thumb of each hand holding the cellophane about three quarters of an inch away from the notch on each side. Without the notch, however, it requires superhuman strength to tear the tube. Give the un-gimmicked half to the sucker, keeping the notched half for yourself. Challenge him to tear his half as you once again unashamedly summon the aid of the notch in tearing yours apart. The sucker will be struggling with his all the way to Havana and back!

Flopover

"As crooked as a dog's hind leg."

For this, equip yourself with an empty matchbox, the type with a label on both sides. Place the box on the edge of the table, with about a third protruding. Using only one finger, you then slowly lever the box up to an upright position. Perhaps not surprisingly, it stands there. You then pass the box to the sucker and challenge him to do the same. However carefully he lifts the box with his finger, he will fail. The box will topple over every time.

Why should the box stand to attention for you and not for your victim? Merely see to it that when you place the box down for yourself, the bottom of the inner drawer is nearer the table. When you place it over the edge for the victim, make sure that the drawer is upside down. The extra weight on top causes the box to topple. When that weight is shifted underneath, it exerts a stabilising influence. Carnival pitchmen have been known to work the swindle with a full box of matches with a coin hidden between the bottom of the drawer and the sleeve to achieve the additional weight. It works just as well, but this version leaves you clean. Should your empty box not have enough extra weight distributed in the case of the drawer, simply wedge a piece of match where the coin would go.

Twister

"I take no fol-de-rol from any man, much less any fiddle-faddle."

The above title is somewhat ambiguous. It could refer either to you or to the elastic band which enables you to perpetrate the swindle. The band should be at least a quarter inch wide. Hold it as shown in the first illustration, which shows your hands from your point of view. Your right thumb (in the loop) and forefinger (outside) hold it at the top, while your left forefinger (in the loop) and thumb (outside) hold it at the bottom. Then, by sliding your right thumb and forefinger in opposite directions, as indicated by the arrows, impart two twists to each side of the band. The result is shown in the second illustration.

The challenge with which you now present yourself is to remove the twists by changing the positions of the hands, but without altering the grip between both thumbs and

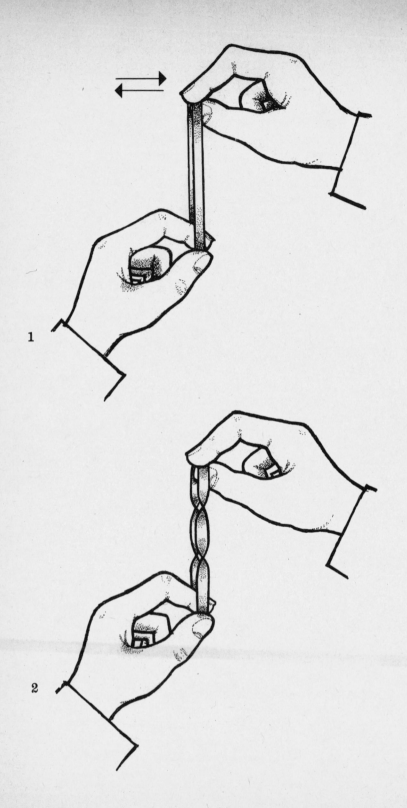

1

2

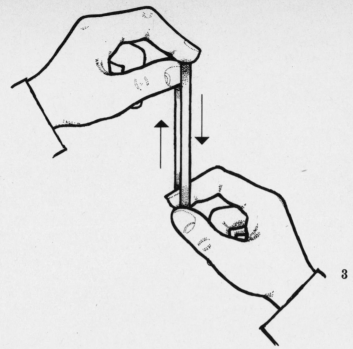

3

forefingers at either end. Simply move your right and left hands in opposite directions past each other until you arrive at the position shown in the third illustration. The twists will melt away. Reverse the positions of the hands to bring yourself back to the second illustration.

Instruct the victim to take the top of the band from your right thumb and forefinger between his own right thumb and forefinger, and the lower end from your left thumb and forefinger likewise in his left hand. Stress that he is now in exactly the same position as you were in the second illustration. At least, that is what he should be led to think! Topologically his situation, because of the left-right reversal as he faces you, is far more involved. Challenge him to get rid of the twists as you did by reversing his hands, lowering the right hand and raising the left at the same time. When he does so, however scrupulously he follows your own moves, the twists, far from melting, double themselves, four on each side of the hand. It is impossible for him to rid himself of the twists without altering his grip. When he gives up, carefully take the band back from him and show him how easy it is.

Hexagon

The following coin puzzle lends itself admirably to the "you-do-as-I-do" motif of this section. You lay out six coins of equal value in two rows of three as shown, openly numbering the coins from 1 to 6. You then show how by moving only three coins, 4, 5 and 1, in that order, you can transform the rows into a near perfect hexagon. You do this several times, each time saying out loud the numbers of the coins moved, namely 4, 5, 1. Make sure that on the completion of the moves 4 touches 5 and 6; 5 touches 1 and 2; and that 1 fits snugly in the gap between 5 and 4, touching them both.

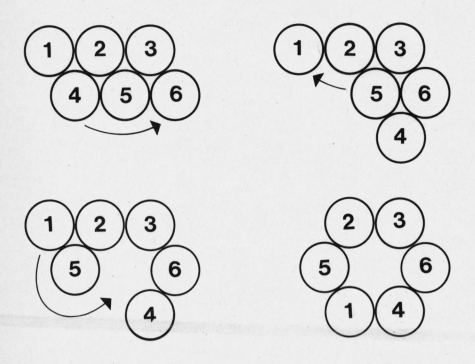

You then challenge the sucker to emulate what you have been showing him. Needless to say, he fails. The reason why he fails is that before he starts you arrange the two rows for him as in the following illustration. As far as he will remember, the lay-out looks the same as before, and you count them from 1 to 6 the same way as before, but he will be unable to make the hexagon unless he imagines the moves in mirror-image.

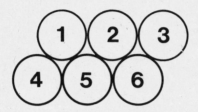

He'll move the coin designated 4 down to touch 5 and 6. Then as he slides out 5 it will gradually dawn upon him – if it hasn't already – that you are cleverer than he thought you were. And that is exactly what you want him to think.

Hydra

"It is impossible to find twelve fair men in all the world."

The confidence trickster who could these days get away with using a double-headed penny in tossing a coin would require the shameless effrontery of a Geller. Disguise the principle, however, and he could well find himself on the scent of even better propositions.

Take ten coins of similar value, one of which must be a double-header. If you are adept at sleight-of-hand, borrow the coins and sneakily switch one for your fake. Hand five to the sucker and keep five, including the double-header, for yourself. You both count your coins, ostensibly to check that you have five each, surreptitiously to ensure that your double-header is second from the top of your pile. You now instruct the victim to "follow your leader"

Everything you do, he is to do in unison with you:
1 Turn all the coins in the pile head upward.
2 Turn the top coin over and place underneath the pile.
3 Take the next coin and without turning it place it underneath.
4 Again turn the next coin over and place it at the bottom of the pile.
5 Again take the next coin and without turning it place it at the bottom.
6 Turn the whole pile over.
7 Turn the top coin over and replace on top.
8 Turn the whole pile over again.
9 Turn the top coin over and replace on top.
10 Turn the whole pile over a last time.
11 Count the coins out in a row on the table and show how all five coins should be back as they were at the start, all heads upward.

At least *yours* will be heads upward! His will come out head, head, tail, head, head, whereupon he scratches *his* head and you cunningly get rid of the incriminating evidence.

Mismatch

"Never mind what I tell you to do – do what I tell you."

This is another adaptation of the principle used in Hydra. The secret is the same, but at the same time less familiar and therefore better. Most people have heard of a double-headed penny, but have you heard of a double-headed matchbox?

The box should resemble the one used in "flopover" in that it should have a label on both sides. Remove the drawer from the sleeve and with a razor blade cut it carefully into two across its centre width. You now re-assemble the matchbox but reverse one half of the drawer in the process. If you now open the box at one end by about a third it will appear the correct way up; open it from the other end and the drawer will appear upside down. Fill this zig-zag drawer with matches and you are ready to bilk the world once more.

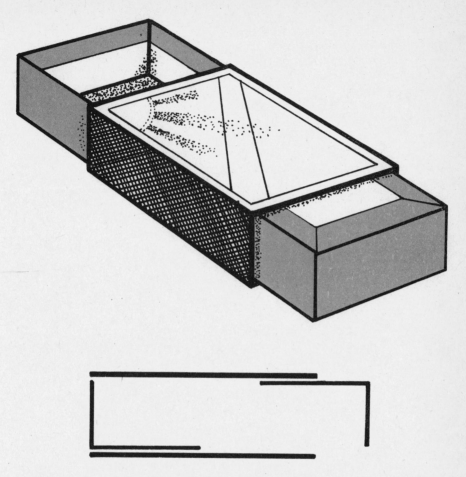

You will also need an ungimmicked matchbox of the same design. This one goes to the sucker. You cling to the "double-header". As in Hydra, he must follow your actions exactly.

1 Open the box so that the matches are showing. (You will have to acquaint yourself with which end of yours is which. Also make sure that the matches in both boxes lie about equally in both directions; you do not want all the striking heads at one end of the box.)
2 Close the box.
3 Turn it over sideways.
4 Turn it over lengthways.
5 Again turn it over sideways.
6 Open the box and take out a match.

This is where the sucker trips up. Your box is the right way up, but his will be upside down, the bottom of his drawer a barrier between him and his matches. Repeat as often as you dare.

Odds That Aren't What They Seem

A compendium of what purport to be – unless otherwise stated – seemingly even-money bets which are in actuality biased remuneratively towards the operator. The latter, when desiring merely to demonstrate their effectiveness, should equip himself with a heap of coins which he distributes evenly between himself and the supposed sucker. If he persists in making sufficient plays, the total amount will soon perforce accrue back to his own person.

Dicey

Singing above the rattle of dice: "Bringing in the sheaves/Bringing in the sheaves/We will come rejoicing ... A hundred and twenty dollars, a hundred and twenty-five, a hundred and thirty ..."

Dice, or the "galloping dominoes" as Fields would have called them, lend themselves especially well to paradoxical proposition bets which appear to offer an even, if not better than even chance, but do in fact give the hustler a marginal edge over his victim. For an encyclopaedic breakdown of the exact percentages of each possible combination of falls one should consult Scarne. Here are just a few such bets that offer you a better than average return as even-money propositions.

Begin with two dice and bet someone that he will roll both a 6 and an 8, before he rolls two 7's. The sucker will reason that since there are six ways to make a 7 and only five ways to make either a 6 or 8, a 7 is obviously easier to roll than either of the other two numbers, and therefore he must be on to a good thing. In fact the bet is far from in his favour, being almost two to one in yours.

Equip yourself with a third die for the next proposition. You keep one and give the other two to your victim. You propose that before he rolls his dice, you will place your die with a specific number showing. If, after his roll, the spots on any two or on all three dice then total seven, you win. If not, you lose. You stress that you can have no idea of how the other two dice will fall when you place your own die down. Regardless of this, however, provided that you make sure your die shows an ace (or 1 spot), your chances of winning will be five out of nine. Repeat this as often as you dare, then hand him the third die. Explain now that when he rolls all three, if a seven shows on any two dice or on all three, *he* will win. In effect you have turned the bet around, but by the end of the day, the sucker will still have lost more than half the total number of throws.

Finally, add two more dice to make five. Declare aces or 1-spots wild, and then bet that if the sucker rolls a pair, he wins. If he rolls three-of-a-kind, he loses. He will reason that since it is more difficult to roll three-of-a-kind than a pair, your offer is more than advantageous. What he will overlook is the fact that it is *easier* to roll three-of-a-kind than a pair with aces wild, incredible as it may sound. *Without* aces wild, the odds against throwing three-of-a-kind amongst five dice are 5·5 to one against, while only 1·2 to one against throwing a pair. On the other hand, *with* aces wild, the odds against three-of-a-kind are 2·2 to one against, while against a pair they are surprisingly 5·5 to one, more than twice as much.

Serial

Man: Would you like to make a few honest dollars for
       yourself?
W.C.: Do they have to be honest?

On American radio many years ago, the Arthur Murray Dancing School offered twenty-five dollars worth of dancing lessons to anyone who could find in his wallet a bill of which the eight digit serial number contained a 2, a 5 or a 7. It was, in fact, a device to get as many people as possible onto the dance floors of the country since the odds of any one of three specific digits appearing is as high as seventeen to one in your favour.

If you think that's too high for you to offer even money on the proposition, merely specify two digits. The odds will still favour you, at five to one. Alternatively, you can bet the sucker that before he removes the dollar bill or pound, (both carry eight digits), he will not be able to name any three of the digits in his serial number. The odds are still healthily on your side.

You can present all the above propositions as even money bets. In this last one, however, you offer to pay him at two to one in his favour. State that you will pay him, say, ten pence if all eight digits on his note are different, provided that he pays you five if two or more are the same. Don't get dizzy, but the odds here favour you at fifty to one!

Sandwich

W.C.: Ever bet on the races?
Man: No, I never wager.
W.C.: You never wager. It's not a bad idea. It's a good system.

This simple proposition can be used as a prelude to a series of coin bets of the more conventional "heads-or-tails" genre. You challenge the sucker that in guessing the date of a coin, any coin, which you are going to ask him to bring at random from his pocket, you will be closer to accuracy than he will. You explain that he will have one guess, while you have two, but to make up for that slight advantage not only can he call first, but you will bet him at two to one. Only after the calls have been made will he bring the coin into view.

Let us suppose that he calls 1961. This means that you must call the two years that sandwich it in time, namely 1960 and 1962. In spite of your allowing him two to one in his favour, the odds are actually something like twelve to one in yours.

Heads-or-Tails

" 'Tain't a fit night out for man or beast."

The "heads-or-tails" motif is in all probability the oldest in the history of gambling. Archaeologists have deduced that flat pebbles from the Old Stone Age found in the caves of Maz d'Azil, France, with a design painted on one side only, were used for primitive betting purposes bordering on divination; maybe with propositions like this one.

You show eight coins and ask the victim how many heads he thinks are likely to turn up if each coin is tossed individually. Normally he will reason to himself – or you can, in fact, spell it out for him – that since there is a fifty-

fifty chance of either a head or tail falling with each coin, with eight coins it would seem most likely to end up with four heads. You then make your offer, namely that you will give him odds of two to one that he will *not* get four heads. He will, no doubt, question your sanity, especially since four heads will tend to turn up more often than any other single number of heads. What he will overlook, however, is that your own interest rests in *any* of the other combinations, giving odds in your favour of eight to three. Four heads will tend to score more often than, say, three heads, but four heads will not score more often than *either* one, two, three, five, six, seven *or* eight heads!

Another similar play upon odds uses just three coins.

Spell out to your victim that there are four ways in which the coins can fall, namely all heads, all tails, two heads and one tail, or two tails and one head. Explain to him that if they fall either all heads or all tails, he wins and you will pay him two coins of whatever value you are using. If they fall the other way, he must pay you, but he need only pay you a single coin. In appearances you are offering him an even chance of winning, but payment which is two to one in his favour. In fact the odds against him are three to one, since on closer inspection you will find that there are actually six ways in which coins can fall in a combination of heads and tails, even though the ratio of two of one symbol to one of the other appears the same in each case.

Spinner

"I'm like Robin Hood – I take from the rich and give to the poor – us poor."

The attraction of the preceding item rests in the fact that the odds favour you without recourse to the standard cliché of coin-tossing, namely the double-headed or double-tailed coin. It would be difficult to get away with the conventional use of such a well-worn gimmick today, although the game Turnover described elsewhere in this volume disguises that principle in your favour. There are, however, other gaffed coins in this area with which the public is far less familiar.

You can purchase from magical supply houses coins with edges which have been bevelled in such a way that when spun on a hard smooth surface they will infallibly fall heads or tails accordingly. If the coin is meant to fall to reveal heads, the bevel will slope towards that side of the coin. The illustration reveals the principle in profile.

Another gimmick, one which you can more easily make for yourself, involves cutting a slight nick with a sharp knife along the edge of a coin on one side. This enables you to challenge anyone that you can tell whether a coin will fall heads or tails when spun behind your back, preferably

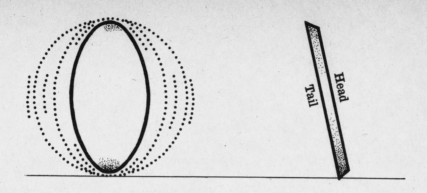

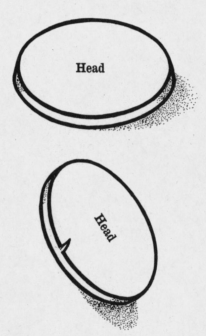

on a wooden surface. You merely listen intently to the way it stops spinning. It it stops abruptly, you know it has fallen onto the side with the notch. If, on the other hand, the spinning subsides more gradually, the nicked side will be uppermost. Experiment will best identify the contrast in sound, as no two "nicked" coins will be exactly alike.

Penney

Prior to meeting legendary gambler, Nick The Greek: "Heads it is. Nicholas Andrea Dandolos, I am ready."

In October 1969, there appeared in the *Journal of Recreational Mathematics*, a problem based on an amazing, but little known fact discovered by the aptly named mathematician, Walter Penney. Given the situation whereby in tossing a coin three times in succession you have one chance in eight of hitting any one of the eight possible sequences, namely, HHH, TTT, HHT, TTH, HTT, THH, HTH, THT, it is possible, whichever combination the sucker himself chooses to bet upon in advance, to choose one for yourself which is more likely to appear first in a random series of tosses. For example, if the chosen combinations were HHT and THH, and the coin fell successively THTHH, THH would win. The odds are always in your favour.

The mathematics of the principle were explained in his usual meticulous detail by Martin Gardner in the October 1974 edition of *Scientific American,* to which the interested reader is referred. For the purposes of play, however, it is sufficient merely to learn the following formula. Whichever combination the sucker calls, to obtain one which will bring the odds into your favour, mentally drop his last symbol, and then put in front of the two symbols left the opposite of the last of that pair. So if he calls HHT, drop the T giving you HH, then add in front of that the opposite of H, namely THH.

The odds in your favour work out as follows:

1 He calls HHH, you call THH, and obtain odds of seven to one in your favour.
2 He calls HHT, you call THH, with odds of three to one.
3 He calls HTH, you call HHT, with odds of two to one.
4 He calls HTT, you call HHT, with odds of two to one.
5 He calls THH, you call TTH, with odds of two to one.
6 He calls THT, you call TTH, with odds of two to one.
7 He calls TTH, you call HTT, with odds of three to one.
8 He calls TTT, you call HTT, with odds of seven to one.

As you can see, the very worst odds you can get are still two to one in your favour! *Whichever* sequence of three the sucker selects, there will always be one left which will give you the winning edge in play.

Payline

Air Hostess: *Are you air sick?*
W.C.:   *No. Somebody put too many olives in my martini*
             last night.

Find seven identical small pay envelopes, the kind that will hold a playing card snugly. In the first five you place a picture card, in the last two a spot card. You then bet the sucker that when the envelopes are shuffled and laid out on the table in a line he will not be able to point to three picture cards in three tries.

Because of the way in which you explain the procedure as a preliminary, the odds do appear to be in his favour. Initially he has five chances in seven of pointing to a picture. Once he has got one, the chances of a second are four in six, and then three in five to secure the third. "In your favour all the way", you spiel. In spite of your reasoning, however, and your offer of even money regardless, he invariably fails to land a lucky trio. In fact, the odds are two and half to one against him.

The same principle coupled with the fallacious reasoning can be adapted in many ways. One novel variation involves the use of a small opaque bottle and seven olives, two of which are green, five black. The green ones are considered the "unlucky" ones. Place all seven olives in the bottle, the neck of which should be of such a size that it will allow only one olive to pass through at a time. Ask the sucker to shake them and then wager that he will not be able to roll out three olives without getting an unlucky green one amongst them. If a green olive shows, he loses. Your explanation of his chances of winning are the same as above: five to two that the first olive will be black, then four to two for the second, finally three to two for the third. Again you bet merely even money, but the odds are still two and a half to one in your favour.

Cartomancy

"I'll bend every effort to win . . . and I come from a long line of effort benders."

More proposition bets have been devised with cards than with any other gambling tool. It might stagger you to learn that some of the following odds favour you so much; but rest assured, they are accurate.

Have the pack shuffled and then cut into three face-down heaps and then offer to bet that there is no picture card on top of any pile. The more astute victim will reason that since there are only twelve picture cards in the pack you are, at even money, giving yourself a considerable advantage. While he hesitates, you declare a change of plan and offer to bet instead on the possibility that a picture card *will* appear. With his mind working backwards, he will now reason that the proposition favours him. In fact you will find the odds approximately six to five in your favour.

You can enlarge them, of course, by increasing the number of piles. With four piles the odds are two to one that a picture card will show. Alternatively, you can include the aces in the same category as the picture cards, in which case the odds are only slightly less than two to one that you will hit a winning card with only three piles.

Have the cards gathered and reshuffled, then spread them face-down on the table. Bet your victim that he won't turn up any four of a kind nominated by himself in any thirty-nine cards. This also works two to one in your favour.

You can secure approximately the same odds with another wager which this time makes use of two shuffled packs. Offer to bet that as you deal cards simultaneously from the top of each pack, two identical cards will appear together at the same position before you have exhausted all 104 cards. In your spiel, you shamelessly "explain" to the sucker that it is "obviously a fifty-fifty proposition since the chance of matching two cards is one in fifty-two and there are fifty-two chances". Usually they fall for it.

A similar "two-together" proposition can be made with a single pack by cutting it into two piles of twenty-six cards, and offering even money that two matching cards of the same colour, say the eight of hearts and the eight of diamonds, will appear simultaneously. The odds remain about the same.

A different kind of "two-together" bet involves asking someone to name two values, disregarding suits, say "ace" and "five" and wagering that in spite of his free choice an ace and a five will arrive together side-by-side in the shuffled pack. He shuffles, then checks by spreading the cards out on the table. Here the odds are three to two in your favour, although you can edge up that advantage by asking instead for a value and a suit, say "three" and "diamond". The odds will then be three to one to your good that on spreading you will find a three adjacent to a diamond. The fact that there are only four cards of one value causes people to overlook the eight chances that exist for any one of the other twelve cards of the specified suit to arrive on either side of a value card. Less favourable, but still giving you odds of five to three, is the bet that two red or two black cards of matching value will find themselves nestling together in the shuffled pack.

Matrimony

"Marriage is a two-way proposition, but never let the woman know she is one of the ways."

Long ago a tradition persisted amongst Soviet peasant girls whereby one would hold six long blades of grass in her fist and extend them to another to tie the six top ends into three pairs, and then the six bottom ends in a similar fashion. If her tying resulted in one continuous loop of grass, the second girl would according to superstition marry within the year.

The odds did in fact favour the prospect of matrimony, the chances of obtaining a single loop being eight in fifteen. If you substitute lengths of string for grass you can easily adapt this principle as a betting stunt. Ask the victim to tie both the upper ends and the lower ends in pairs at random. He loses if he produces the continuous loop. To increase the odds in your favour, discard two strings. With only four in hand, you are likely to win two times out of three.

71

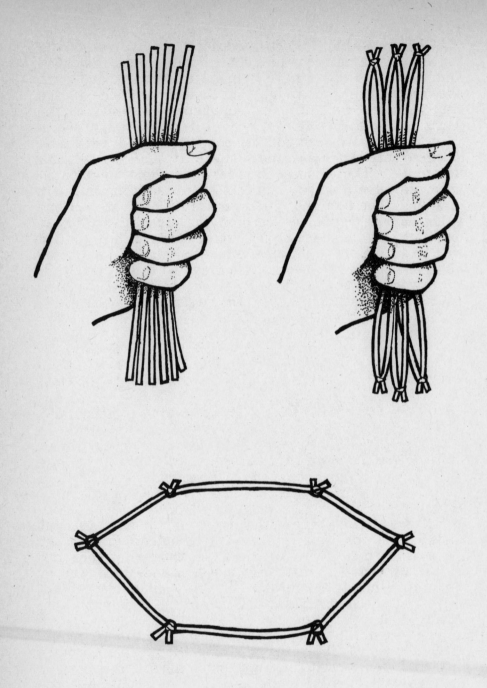

Googol

"Shall we have another wager?" And then, as the gambler reaches for his gun – "Probably at some future day!"

You will need nine slips of paper and a pencil. Hand everything to your opponent with instructions that on each slip he write at random a different number. He can go as low as one, as high as a googol, namely one followed by a hundred zeros. The only stipulation you make is that he should not write either two consecutive numbers, or the same number twice. Also you must not see what he writes. When he has finished he is to place the slips number sides down on the table. Then you make your bet. You will start turning over the slips at random and even though you have no idea of what numbers he wrote, you wager that you will stop turning on the highest number.

Simply remember to turn over any three slips without stopping, then carry on turning until you reach a number higher than the highest figure in the first three. Stop there. If you find yourself turning all the slips, you must stop at, and therefore choose, the last one turned. This system gives you the maximum odds of winning which are just over one in three. Obviously to be certain of making an overall profit the spectator must pay you at odds of two to one, but since the object is to find one number amongst as many as nine, most people will suppose that to be fair.

Birthday

"I'd rather have two girls at twenty-one each than one girl at forty-two."

For this you will have to pick the right occasion, ideally a gathering of no less than thirty people, not including yourself. Assuming that number is present, bet the sucker that there will be two people in the room who share the same birthday (month and day that is, disregarding year). The less well you know the people, the more likely he will be to rise to your bait. Obviously, it must not look as if you have had an opportunity to check dates with everyone beforehand. When one considers that there are as many as 366 possible days to choose from, the probability does seem remote. Yet on an even money basis you have a much better chance of winning than losing.

If you were to attempt this with different groups of thirty people, you would be likely to win approximately seven times out of every ten. The more people, the better your odds, until with about sixty (still few by comparison with 366) individuals, you are bordering close on certainty. To have an absolute 100% guarantee you would need 367 people present, but, of course, the least likely occurrence in all this is that you would ever need them! If you doubt these figures, you only have to check them out with any thirty names picked at random from *Who's Who* or any other biographical dictionary.

Dicing with the Future

In which the mountebank assumes the meretricious mantle of a clairvoyant in determining the successful conclusion of his wager.

Oddity

"Ladies and gentlemen – Brentwood is the smallest giant in the world – whilst his brother Elwood is the largest midget."

The items in this section fall into a special category, the secrets of which are so simple that it would appear utterly impossible for anyone to be hoodwinked by them – until, that is, they are put into practice. This challenge can be performed at the shortest notice with matches, coins, pebbles, even the spots on dice. It all comes down to numbers in the end.

For the purposes of explanation, assume it takes the form of a dice game. You will also need a cup or, failing that, the drawer of a matchbox with which to cover one die. Give that die to the victim, asking him to roll it without your seeing and then to cover it with the cup. When he has done so, you deliver your wager. You claim that you also will put down a die, this time with a number showing, and you guarantee that whatever number he has rolled, the sum of your number added to his will total the opposite of his number. In other words, if he has rolled odd, adding your number to his must make it even for you to win. Alternatively, if he rolled even, that added to yours must produce odd. You always succeed.

How? Because you only ever put down an odd number! If he rolls even, say 4, adding either 1, 3, or 5 to it will give an opposite odd total, either 5, 7, or 9 respectively. But likewise, if he rolls odd, say 5, still adding either your 1, 3, or 5, again produces an opposite, in this case even, total, either 6, 8, or 10.

In explaining the object of the game to your victim, you can throw him off the scent psychologically by quoting false examples. If, you spiel, he puts down a 4, and you then put down a 6, you lose, he wins, because his even number stays even. Similarly, if he puts down a 3 and you put down a 2, he wins again, because his odd number stays odd. Remember that if you do place down an even number he *will* win.

Each time you do win, you can always appear to commiserate with him, by turning your die to a number that would have meant your losing. So, if you put down a 1, converting his, say, 4 successfully to odd, you could then turn your die over to 2 with a line like, "You see how close you came. If I had put down a 2, your number would still be even, and you would have won." You can even set your number down first and cover your die. Make out that it all hinges on whether you put an odd or even number, whether you win or lose. The chances look even, but your dice might as well be loaded, so completely is the ruse in your favour.

Certainty

W.C.: Son, do you doubt my unimpeachable integrity? Do you think I would resort to a tarradiddle? Do you think I would tell a downright fib?
Son: Yes.

Another twist of the same principle. Take a full pack of cards from their case leaving the joker behind, then ask the sucker to cut the pack into seven piles. You stress that he could arrive at an odd or an even number of cards in any one pile. Before he commences the cuts, however, you bet him that he will end up with an odd number of piles containing an *even* number of cards. He cuts, counts, and checks. You win.

Gather the cards and start to return them to their case, then as an afterthought offer to repeat the bet. By this time you have secretly added the joker to the pack. That you now have fifty-three cards means that you can adjust the bet, which should now state that when he cuts the pack into seven piles, the number of piles containing an *odd* number of cards will be odd. It works every time.

Milady

W.C.:   *Whom have I the honour of addressing, Milady?*
Mae West: *They call me Flower Belle.*
W.C.:   *Flower Belle! What a euphonious appellation!*

Everyone has heard of the three card trick. In this, however, you attempt something even more remarkable, namely the *seven* card trick. Not only that, but you "find the lady" without even looking at the cards. Moreover, so sure are you of your challenge that you substitute the seventh card, the queen, for a pound note. Should you fail to find the pound you forfeit it; should you succeed, the drinks certainly should not be on you.

Ask the victim to take six spot cards from a pack, and add the pound note to the cards. Turn aside so that you are prevented from getting a glimpse of the action; then give him the following instructions. Tell him to:

1 Mix the cards and the pound note and place them in a straight row on the table in any order.
  He must not tell you where he places the pound.
2 Note the position held by the pound in the row. He may count from either end.
3 He must now rearrange the position of the cards and pound by a series of moves. You must make clear to him the exact definition of a "move". One "move" always consists of changing the position of the pound with one, only one, of the cards on either side of it. Should the pound arrive at the end of the row, there will obviously be only one card with which to arrange it, and therefore only one way in which to "move". First he must make a number of "moves" equal to the position held by the pound in step 2.
4 Make another "move" with the pound, and then another.
5 Now discard the 2 cards at each end of the row.
6 Make three "moves" with the pound
7 Again discard the 2 end cards.
8 Make one "move" with the pound.
9 Now discard the card on the far left.
10 Make one final "move" with the pound.
11 Again discard the card on the far left.

There will be one piece of paper left. The pound note!

Turnover

Man : There's been a mistake in my change.
*W.C.: Ah, at long last, an honest man – you want to return
 some money?*
Man : No, I'm short.
W.C.: Don't brag about it. I'm only 5 feet 8 inches myself.

In this challenge the "heads-or-tails" motif is passed
through a pseudo-telepathic dimension to your advantage.
There is no casual coin-tossing here. Everything appears
far more scientifically (?) controlled.

Ask the sucker to reach into his pocket and place a
handful of change on the table. While your back is turned,
instruct him to turn over at random two coins at a time as
many times as he likes, as quietly as possible. Each
successive double-turn is completely independent of the
others. It doesn't matter if the same coin is included in the
double-turning procedure twice, or even more times, in
succession. When he is satisfied that he has turned them
over enough times, he must cover one coin, any coin, with
his hand. Only then do you turn around and immediately
declare your interest: "I bet you the value of that coin
that, no matter how often you have turned it over, it is now
head up." He removes his hand and you pocket the coin.

There is no way you can predict what coins he is going to
turn, what coin he is going to cover, points which your
pitchman's patter should emphasise to him. What you
don't tell him, though, is that before you turn your back on
him, you quickly note whether the number of coins showing *heads* is odd or even. An absence of heads showing
counts as even. If he then follows your instructions for
double-turning the coins, when he stops, if he started with
an odd number of heads, he will still have an odd number.
Likewise, if there had been an even number of heads showing originally, he will end up with an even number. Without
knowing this, he covers one of the coins. You turn back,
again secretly count the heads showing, and using simple
mental arithmetic, tell him whether he is concealing
heads or tails.

Humm-dinger

"For those who are continually embarrassed by the conventional squabble for the restaurant check, I'd advise this: when it comes to the point where, inevitably, the other person says, 'Now let's not fight about this,' just answer 'Very well, old man.' Remember, the complete gentleman never brawls."

This perplexing challenge has undergone many transformations since it emanated from the brain of its inventor, Bob Hummer, a master of the subtle yet intriguing solution. To gain the fullest impact from the principle with a gambling presentation, you will need three tea cups and a pound note or dollar bill.

The cups are turned mouth downwards on the table in a row. Roll the pound into a ball, and balance it on the bottom of one of them. You then make your wager. No matter under which cup the victim places the pound, you will find it first time. Should you fail, he can take the note. Turn aside and only then tell him to place the pound under a cup of his choice. When he has done this he is to switch around the positions of the other two empty cups in order, you say, to confuse you. You turn back and lift one cup. Out rolls the crumpled pound. This you repeat time after time.

Ideally the cups should come from the same set and appear similar. Examine the bottoms of any three such cups carefully and you will find chips, scratches, blemishes, which will act as identifying marks to each one. If you are presented on the spur of the moment with any three cups, a brief glance will single out one blemish as more easily recognisable than the others. The cup with this mark becomes your key cup. This is the principle upon which the whole challenge is based.

Decide quickly upon your key cup before turning aside and remember its position in the row. When you turn back after the pound has been hidden and the cups have been moved, a simple process of deduction will lead you to the pound. If the key cup is still in the same position, then obviously it was not switched around. Therefore it must hide the pound. On the other hand, should it not be in the same position, then it must have been switched. In which case the pound note will neither be under the key cup nor under the cup which is in the position the key cup originally held. That leaves one cup. Lift it and there is the pound.

You don't, of course, have to use a pound note. The next time you are in a restaurant and you arrive at that embarrassing lull in *bonhomie* when it must be decided who is to pay the bill, crumple the latter into a ball and with three cups proceed on the following conditions with the above challenge. If you uncover the bill first time, they pay; if you don't find it, you pay. You'll never go hungry!

Jackpot

"If a thing's worth having, it's worth cheating for!"

Start saving all your odd pennies until you have in excess of one hundred. The exact number is immaterial, although the more you are able to hoard, the more impressive the gamble will eventually appear. Keep them together in a paper bag, metal bowl or some other container which allows of easy access. This is your "jackpot".

When you are ready to bluff the world, choose your unsuspecting victim and explain the jackpot to him. Turn aside, emphasising that you would not cheat by looking, and ask him to reach into the hoard and bring out in his clenched fist any number of coins, provided that they do not exceed, say, twelve pence. He must keep his hand closed for the time being. Turn back and yourself reach into the jackpot and grasp a handful, though make sure that you have, in this example, comfortably more than twelve, the maximum he could have taken. Now, making scrupulously sure that neither of you can *see* or *hear* the other, count your coins to yourselves. You are then ready to make your wager. The challenge is for you to tell him exactly how many coins he has in his hand. If you are right, he must give you, from his own pocket, a sum equal in value to that which he is holding. If you are wrong, he can take the jackpot.

Needless to say, you never forfeit your nest-egg. Your security is locked into the wording of your statement, something like, "I wager that I hold as many coins as you, four more, and enough to make your sum fifteen pence."

You then ask the sucker to name his total. Suppose he says he has eight pence. From your own pile, count off eight – his number; then count off the "four more"; pause, then conclude, "and remember I said I had enough left over to make your sum fifteen pence". Then proceed to count, after reaffirming that he did have eight, "Nine, ten, eleven, twelve, thirteen, fourteen", and then with a triumphant final flourish on the precise final number, "fifteen".

So far, so confusing! But all you have to do is to make sure that you take a larger number of coins than the victim. Hence the specimen number stipulated in the second paragraph. When you first count yours to yourself, the last thing you are thinking of is the number the victim actually took. Merely count off to yourself a small, arbitrary number of coins – say, five – and then count the rest, which we'll suppose to be seventeen. You would then say, on the pattern of the above, "I have as many coins as you, five more, and enough to make yours seventeen." Given that you have made sure that you hold that many *more* coins than he does anyhow, of course you have *as many as* he has, and of course you can make his sum up to seventeen. The dimple throw-off phrase "five more" is total misdirection. So when you count out loud, you count to the spectator's number, the one he has just told you, then deliver the throw-off, and finally continue counting to your main sum of seventeen. So if the victim had nine pence, you would count up to nine, then resume the count on ten.

Once you have grasped the principle, you will realise how simple it is, so simple that you will query whether anyone could possibly be taken in by it. To prove its perplexity, however, you will have to try it out for yourself. The more you repeat it, varying the "throw-off number" each time, the more confusing it becomes to the victim, a situation helped by the endless variations you can play on the theme. Above, the victim takes his coins before you, but there is no reason why you can't go first. You can count yours and announce your wager, before he counts his. You can get him merely to think of a sum, and yet still you win. No less than the late Al Koran, the suave English mentalist/magician, who enjoyed a considerable vogue in the fifties, used to feature a version of this swindle in his stage act. He announced it as "The trick that baffled Einstein." Which only goes to prove that even scientists can be suckers.

The Classic Swindles

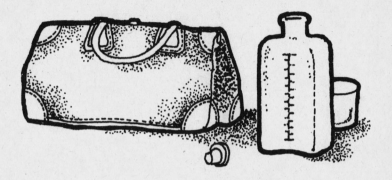

Being a self-contained folio of those dodges and wiles which by virtue of their oft repeated success have bestowed greatest distinction upon the noble art of cozenage.

Spot

"If at first you don't succeed, try, try again. Then quit. No use being a damn fool about it."

This piece of hanky-panky is right in the van of the mainstream tradition of carnival swindles, where the easier and fairer it looks, the harder it becomes. The customer is confronted by a red circular spot measuring five inches in diameter painted on the counter. He is given five flat discs each measuring slightly more than three inches in diameter. The object of the game is to cover the red spot completely using nothing more than the five discs. Obviously the spot is the largest possible that can be legitimately covered by the discs, which must be dropped onto the spot one at a time and, once in position, cannot be moved again. The merest speck of red showing means that the game is lost. Needless to say, the customer loses every time.

There are various methods of fleecing the public with this game. They include painting the spot on oilcloth so that its shape can be subtly distorted by stretching and using a key disc that is itself distorted. Most appealing, however, because of its simplicity, is the simple geometrical approach using ungimmicked props. First have the sucker drop the discs as he thinks fit from a height of about six inches. The slightest deviation from a perfect drop with any one of the discs will spell failure on his part. The probability that a skilled player can drop a disc from that height onto the exact position it should occupy is, according to Scarne, about one in three or two to one against. The probability that he will score five perfect drops can then be computed at one in three[5] or 243! Of course the more attempts he makes the more he'll come to reason along exact geometrical lines. The first illustration, as well as indicating the exact relative proportions of discs and spot, shows the arrangement which most people work out in their minds as the ideal to be achieved.

To climax his series of losses allow him to place the discs down carefully without dropping them. The odds are that he will attempt the arrangement shown in the first illustration with the circumferences of all five discs converging at the centre of the spot. Then let him look

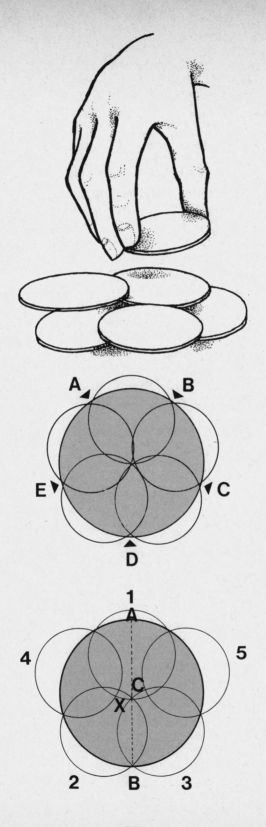

closely and point out – with a magnifying glass if necessary – the minute specks of red around the spot's rim at ABCDE. The second illustration reveals the superior arrangement which you then proceed to show him.

Imagine the diameter AB. First put disc 1 into position, ensuring that its centre rests on AB and that the base of its circumference X is slightly below the centre of the spot, C. Next put down discs 2 and 3 so that their circumferences pass through X and B, whereupon discs 4 and 5 fall obviously into place. The exact measurements for the spot and the discs are respectively 5 inches and 3·045 inches in diameter precisely. The distance CX works out at about 0·07 inch. Nothing less than 3·045 will cover the 5-inch spot as detailed in the winning method. Attempting the first arrangement with discs of this size will automatically result in failure. Using that method you would need discs at least 3·09 inches in diameter to cover the same spot completely.

The goal for which the operator should aim is to be able to effect the second arrangement as rapidly as possible seemingly dropping the discs from a height of six inches, but in fact – by using the misdirection provided by swift up-and-down and back-and-forth movements of the hand – making the drops from no more than about an inch above the spot.

Pentagram

Man: Maybe you're lost.
W.C.: Kansas City is lost; I am here!

This challenge may have originated in Mexico, where it bears the name "Estrella Magica" or "Magic Star". The star in question is the mysterious and legendary five-pointed pentagram which can be drawn in one continuous line without lifting pen from paper. Explain this fact as you draw it and then point out that the star has five points and five intersections, a total of ten spots. The object of the game is to cover all but one of these spots with coins in the following manner. First place a coin on any spot, then move the coin along a line across an intersection and bring it to rest on the next spot. This is repeated with a second coin and a third and so on until nine spots are covered. Each coin must commence at an uncovered spot and finish on an uncovered spot. Each move must jump one intersection, though it does not matter whether this has a coin on it or not. Once a coin comes to rest, it cannot be moved again. You can demonstrate this many times, on each occasion starting your first move from a different spot, yet people are still unable to duplicate your success.

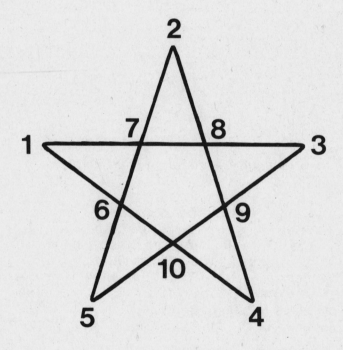

The secret is simple. Your moves follow a basic pattern; each successive coin must end its move on the spot from which you began the preceding move. Assume you place a coin on spot 9 and move it to 2. Your next move is to start at a spot which enables you to move it to 9 itself, namely 5.

The third coin must now end on 5, which means you must start at 7. And so on, until all nine coins are on the star. Here is another example:

First coin   placed on 4, jumps 10, ends on 6
Second coin placed on 8, jumps 9, ends on 4
Third coin   placed on 1, jumps 7, ends on 8
Fourth coin placed on 10, jumps 6, ends on 1
Fifth coin   placed on 3, jumps 9, ends on 10
Sixth coin   placed on 7, jumps 8, ends on 3
Seventh coin placed on 5, jumps 6, ends on 7
Eighth coin placed on 9, jumps 10, ends on 5
Ninth coin   placed on 2, jumps 8, ends on 9

In demonstrating the moves, do so with a blend of swift actions and indecisiveness. Don't always make the move immediately. Appear to be trying other spots first, then finally come back to the correct one.

Morra

"Mayor, you're okay. I voted for you last election – five times."

This is the ancient game played by most people in childhood in which two players, standing back to back if a third party is available, simultaneously extend either one, two or three fingers as they shout the number they guess their opponent has shown. If both guess right or both guess wrong, that round is drawn. If only one guesses right, however, the other has to pay him as many coins as the combined total of the fingers extended at that point in the game.

So far, so innocent, until the mathematician John Von Neumann worked out a strategy which usually enables those acquainted with it to win, or if not to win, at least to break even. Each time you simply "guess", as the number of fingers your opponent is showing, the difference between the number you are showing and four. You also have to make sure that in any twelve rounds you show one finger five times, two fingers four times, three fingers three times. You must make this more haphazard than it reads

You		Sucker
0	'2' → '2'	5
0	'1' '1'	0
0	'3' '3'	0
4	'3' → '2'	0
4	'2' → '1'	0
0	'3' '3'	0
0	'2' ← '2'	5
0	'1' '2'	0
4	'3' → '3'	0
0	'2' '1'	0
4	'3' → '3'	0
0	'1' ⇄ '3' (NO SCORE)	0
16	TOTALS	10

so that it doesn't *look* like a system. This will help to disguise the fact that whenever you extend three fingers, you shout "one", two fingers, "two", one finger, "three". The last thing you want is for the sucker to crack the system; otherwise *he* will beat *you*.

Shortchanged

"I know a thief when I see one. When I was young, I was the biggest thief at large. I'd steal golf balls, piggy banks of dear little kiddies, or nozzles off the hoses of the rectory lawn."

That anyone might be duped into paying money for something which rightfully belongs to him only serves to underline the typically Fieldsian philosophy quoted elsewhere in this book, "Suckers have no business with money anyway." If you don't believe the above proposition is likely, try these for size.

Take a five pound note from your pocket and ask the sucker to match it with one of his own. Fold them together and place them both in a glass. Ask him how much is in the glass. He should reply ten pounds, whereupon you offer to sell him both the glass and the notes for six pounds. If he accepts the deal, as he often will, you will make a pound minus the cost of the glass. People *do* forget that one of the five pound notes was theirs in the first place.

You can try the same thing more cheaply this way. Place three coins of equal value in a row and ask the sucker to match them with three similar coins of his own. Let's imagine the coins are tenpenny pieces. Pocket one of your original coins, and have the sucker do likewise from his row. Then push the four coins left on the table in his direction with the words, "Give me thirty pence for the rest of the coins." You will be surprised how many forget that two of the coins they are buying were theirs originally, "originally" meaning only seconds ago. This time you should be ten pence richer.

Inferno

"I'll teach you when you grow up. I never smoked a cigarette until I was nine."

A popular bar game involves securing a drumhead of tissue paper around the mouth of a tumbler with an elastic band. Both players place a small coin on the centre of the stretched tissue. They also need a cigarette, the lighted end of which they take turns in placing against the tissue, burning a small hole in the process. Play proceeds in rotation. Whoever applies the burn that causes the coins to drop into the glass loses and forfeits the cash.

You play legitimately for a while and then warn your opponent that you have at last figured out his strategy. He will probably sound surprised, since the likelihood is that he hasn't got one. Still, you are so confident of your theory, you claim, that you offer to quadruple the bet. You qualify your statement by adding that if he burns the first hole, you are sure that you yourself will win. Win you do, but not through skilled reasoning or logic. This time you make the drumhead, not out of tissue, but out of flash paper. This can be obtained at any joke shop or magical supply house. It looks like real tissue, feels like real tissue, but bring it into contact with the merest spark and it disappears – flash! – in an instant. Say no more!

Corridor

Mae West: *Two rooms – if you don't mind.*
W.C.: *Yes – The bridal suite. We're married, you know.*
Mae West: *I'll take the suite. Give him the room.*
W.C.: *But, my dove ...*

There were ten people seeking separate rooms in a hotel which had only nine vacant rooms in which to accommodate them. For a small wager you offer to demonstrate how the problem was solved *without* people having to double up.

With a pencil sketch a long rectangle which you then divide into nine squares, each space representing a room.

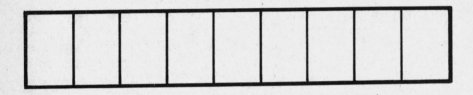

Marking one cross in the first square and another outside, you demonstrate how the first man made his way to the first room, but was overtaken at the door by the second man.

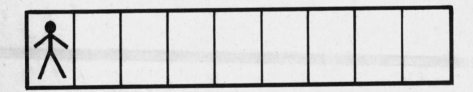

The third man then went into the second room, the fourth into the third and so on until the ninth went into the eighth. Mark each of the seven rooms in the centre with a cross as you count "Third, fourth, fifth, sixth, seventh, eighth, ninth".

At this point there was one vacant room left, whereupon the manager took the extra man still standing outside the first room and led him to the ninth. Circle the cross outside the first room and draw a curve connecting it with the last square, marking the final cross inside as you count "tenth".

Then quickly proceed to *your* room and lock the door!

Dilemma

"Business is an establishment that gives you the legal, even though unethical, right to screw the naïve – right, left, and in the middle."

Have someone place a tenpenny piece of his own on the table and then cover it with any card drawn face-up from the pack. Let's suppose the card is the two of clubs. You bet him five pence that he will *not* answer the value of the card on the table to each of your next three questions.

Begin by asking two completely irrelevant ones. He will be on his guard, expecting a catch, and should answer "the two of clubs" both times. You then ask him what he will take for his coin beneath the card. This places him in a considerable dilemma. He might answer "the two of clubs", in which case you take him at his word, give him the card, pocket the ten pence for yourself and then pay him five pence for winning the bet. You still make five pence out of the transaction. Alternatively, if he refuses to say "two of clubs", he gets his coin back, but has to hand you over five pence for losing the bet. Either way you can't lose. Of course, you can make the stakes higher, if you dare.

Matrix

W.C.:   *May I present my card?*
Mae West: *"Novelties and Notions". What kind of notions you got?*
W.C.:   *You'd be surprised. Some are old and some are new.*

For this game, draw on a piece of paper a five by five grid as shown and then alternate on the squares within the grid thirteen copper coins and twelve silver ones. After the removal of one of the copper coins, you now take turns with an opponent in moving coins of one colour each either up, down, or sideways – but never diagonally – to the one vacant square. The player who eventually finds himself unable to move loses. In fact, provided that you play second, you can always win.

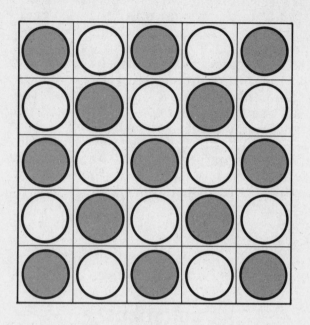

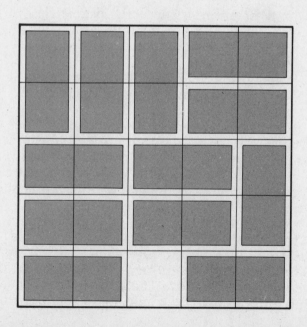

Grant your opponent the courtesy of removing the copper coin of his choice and then to make the first move. He'll have to move a silver coin and this will remain his colour throughout, leaving you with copper. Before you make your first move, however, you have to stretch your imagination. Picture in your mind that the grid – with the exception of the square from which your opponent removed the copper coin – is covered by twelve dominoes. Had the third square in the fifth row been vacated, you might imagine the layout shown in the second illustration. Any arrangement will work, provided that the invisible "dominoes" are not allowed to overlap each other or the original vacant square. Now whenever your opponent moves a silver coin, merely make sure that you move the copper coin that is on the "domino" he has just left. In that way you will always have a move up your sleeve with which to follow his move. In other words, he hasn't a hope of winning.

Columbus

Holding Mae West's arm: "Ah! What symmetrical digits. Soft as the fuzz on a baby's arm."

Although this game is based on a "pairing strategy" similar to that used in Matrix, your imagination can take a rest. Here you use *actual* dominoes.

Two players take it in turns to place dominoes of equal size flat upon a square or rectangle. After one domino is set down it must not be disturbed by the other player. This continues until the square is so crowded that there is no room left for another domino, the winner being the person to place a domino last.

If the first player – you! – places a domino exactly in the centre of the square, all you have to do to ensure eventual victory is to duplicate symmetrically your opponent's play at each successive placing. Refer to the illustration where the numbers indicate the order of play in a sample game. Just make sure that you have enough dominoes, sufficient, in fact, to cover the square completely when they are packed tight edge to edge in conventional lines.

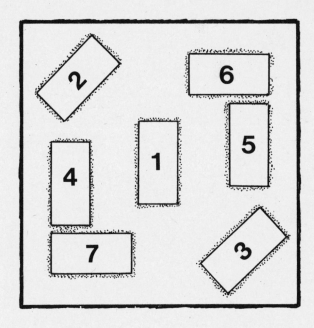

The title? Legend has it that the game was played long ago by Columbus, not with dominoes, but with eggs. In addition to "discovering" America, the explorer was famous for his reputed feat of balancing an egg on end – simply by cracking the wide end slightly, thus flattening the shell into an actual base. Sam Loyd, the American puzzle expert, conjectured that he balanced the egg so that it would stand in the centre of the square (he used a square napkin) in such a game. Only then could he proceed to win the game. By setting it on end he made the egg symmetrical for the purposes of the winning strategy. Unlike the domino, the oval shape of an egg does not retain the same shape when rotated through 180 degrees. Unless the object at the centre can be seen or made to be symmetrical in this fashion you have no guarantee of victory.

Garland

"Somehow, Satan got behind me."

Instruct your opponent to arrange any number of coins in an unbroken circle, each coin touching the two on either side. The object of the game, a sister of Columbus, is to take turns in removing either one coin or an adjoining pair of coins from the circle in such a way that whoever takes the last coin wins.

Provided that you play second – again, as in Matrix, out of courtesy to the sucker who goes first – you can always win. When he makes his first move and thus breaks the circle, just check whether the number of coins left in the arc is odd or even. If odd, for your first move take away the centre coin. If even, take away the two coins at the centre. In either case you will be left with two equal strands of coins. Now whatever move he makes next, you duplicate it from the opposite strand. So if he takes a pair from the strand nearer him, you take a pair from the other. With practice you will be able to make your moves appear less obvious than might sound from this description.

You can vary your strategy by counting from either end of the strand remaining to you, so that in the case of two strands of, say, seven coins, if your opponent removes the second coin from one of them, you could then remove either the second or the sixth from the other. Once again, it's all a question of symmetry.

Buster

"One of my most precious treasures – an exquisite pair of loaded dice, bearing the date of my graduation from high school."

The variety of crooked dice available for illegal gambling purposes is infinite, as the merest glance at *Scarne on Dice*, the definitive work on the subject by America's foremost gambling expert, will show. While it is not easy for the average reader to obtain the elaborately gaffed items detailed in that volume, the dice employed in the following sequence can be constructed by anyone with little trouble.

Special only by virtue of the distribution of their spots, they are known to mechanics variously as "Tops and Bottoms", "Busters", "Ts", and "Mis-Spots". That special distribution is best shown by the illustration which depicts a pair of such dice themselves and their mirror image. One die merely carries the odd numbers, 1, 3, 5, the other the even numbers, 2, 4, 6, in each case with the duplicate numbers on opposite sides to each other.

Hand the dice to the sucker and have him roll them a few times so that he can assure himself they are not loaded. Because he can only see a maximum of three sides on any die at one time, at no point will he be able to see two duplicate sides on any die! He then hands you one die back and depending upon whether this is the odd or the even die, wager that your next roll will produce odd or even accordingly. Repeat, but this time bet the opposite and have *him* roll the other die. Finally hand him the second die back and have him roll both dice together. You wager "odd" – it can only be "odd" – and win again. You've scored your hat trick, stove-pipe of course!

It is advisable to have a pair of straight dice at hand to substitute for the gaffed ones at the conclusion. Should you be challenged, however, you can in fact show that the crooked pair are fair. If they were straight, obviously each pair of opposite sides on each die would total seven. Just put the dice side by side in such a way that they total seven on top and along one of the sides. You can then show that all the other sides, the outer ends, as well as the two sides facing inwards, all total seven. The dice can't be anything but straight! Or can they?

Mosca

On ordering breakfast in the Black Pussy Café: "I don't know why I ever come in here – the flies get the best of everything."

This ancient Spanish game was a great favourite of major-league gambler, Benjamin "Bugsy" Siegel. Legend has it that he would frequently order with his breakfast not only the sugar cubes required, but also a box of the live flies essential for the wager. In this way he would set himself up for sport for the rest of the morning.

All doors and windows in his room would be closed, the air conditioning switched off, then the flies released from their perforated prison. Siegel would unwrap two sugar cubes, position them about six inches apart, and bet his breakfast companion sums to the tune of five thousand dollars that a fly would land on his cube first. He invariably won. One morning in 1947 he had a shrewder opponent in fellow mobster, Willie Moretti. After Siegel had relieved him of five thousand dollars, he only agreed to play again if he could take Siegel's cube. This Siegel agreed and still he won.

Siegel had in fact secretly doctored both cubes beforehand with a drop of DDT on one side. First time around he slyly made sure that the impregnated side of his cube was closest to the table, while that of Moretti's was uppermost. Second time around, under the pretence of moving the cubes further apart, he unobtrusively turned them both over. All so much easier than training flies, the only solution Moretti himself could think of.

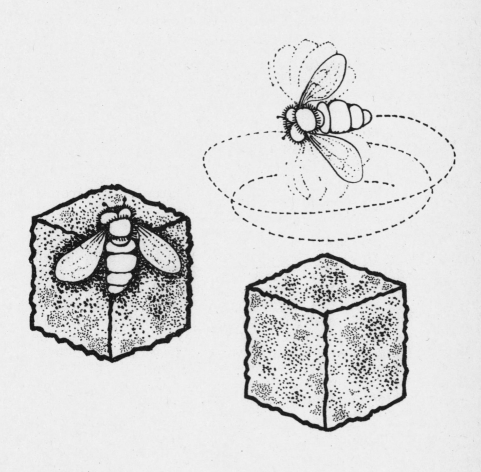

Thirty-one

"I should have gone to night school, then I'd be able to add."

Played extensively in Australia, hence often referred to as the "Australian Gambling Game of 31", this was in fact invented, according to nineteenth-century gambling expert J. H. Green, way back in the dim past by one "Dr Bennett alias Charles James Fox of England" (1749–1806), a statesman and a scholar and notorious as a bad influence on the Prince of Wales!

From a pack of cards remove all the spot cards from ace through to six, twenty-four cards in all, then arrange them on a table as shown in the illustration.

Again the game is for two players. Both take turns in turning one card face-down, adding the values of the cards turned as they do so. Whoever reaches thirty-one first, wins. Once a card is turned face-down it is out of play. Should a player be forced to go over thirty-one, he loses. Have no fear of this, however, because you can win every time, regardless of whoever starts the play, by remembering a simple series of secret key numbers. The sequence is 3, 10, 17, 24, easily remembered as a progression of 7 from 3, i.e. 3, 3+7 or 10, 10+7 or 17, 17+7 or 24.

Should the opponent commence the game by turning over any card higher than 3 in value, turn over a card which will bring the total level with your second key number, which is 10. So, if he turns a 6, you turn a 4. He might then turn a 3, bringing the total to 13, in which case you would turn over another 4 to hit your next key, 17. Suppose he then turns a 1, making a total of 18, you then turn a 6 bringing the sum to 24, the final key. Whatever card he turns next, in no way can he score thirty-one on his next move, whereas you cannot avoid hitting the target on yours.

Should your opponent turn 1 or 2 on his opening move, bring the total to 3, your first key, on yours; should he turn a 3, deliberately play low and strive to hit a key number as soon as possible. For those games where you play first, begin by turning your first key, 3. Whatever your opponent turns second, nothing can prevent you hitting your key numbers in an easy sly stride.

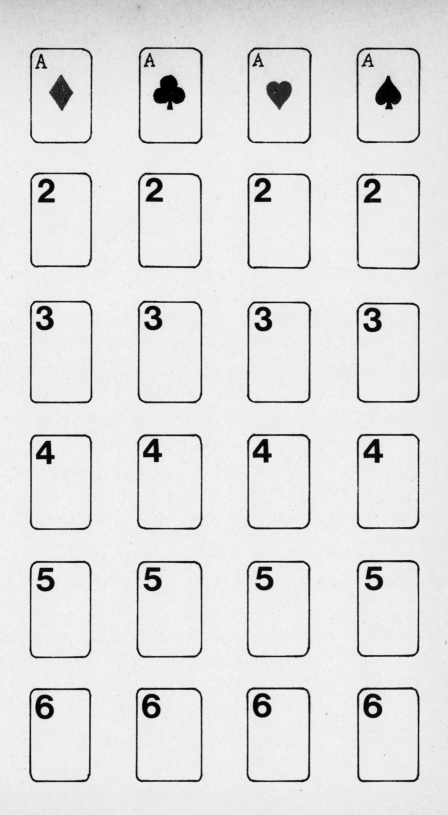

If you persist in playing the game, your opponent will, of course, latch onto the fact that you always start on a 3, or that various numbers, namely your keys, occur with amazing regularity in the totalling. This is where you may, if you wish, explain the whole system to him, how he must always start on a 3, how he must aim to reach the keys. Better still have a "shill" or accomplice take him aside to explain. Now obviously he will feel that with a knowledge of the key numbers, if he turns a 3 first, he must win the game. So he enters another game and this is where the stakes really should climb high. Allow the sucker to being by turning a 3. You follow with another 3 bringing the total to 6. The sucker will now turn 4 to make the first key 10. You follow with another 4, making 14, whereupon he must turn 3 to produce the next key, 17. You then take 3, totalling 20. The sucker adds 4 to this, securing the last key, 24. You follow with another 4, bringing the total to 28, at which the mouth of your opponent should drop to the floor! When he goes to turn a 3 to make 31, he will find that there is no 3 left to turn. He has no choice but to turn a 1 or a 2, playing straight into your hands. Whichever he turns, you then add the other to produce the winning total again of 31. Should he at any point avoid the card you are "forcing" him into turning, don't worry. The path will then be wide open for you to hit a key number yourself.

Nim

"You won't consider me rude if I play with my mitts on, will you?"

Whereas in Garland your winning aim was to pick up the last coin, in the more famous Nim, presumably so called after the Anglo-Saxon verb, *nim*, meaning to take away or steal, it is the picking up of the last object which you must *avoid*.

The game is traditionally played with matches, although coins or any small objects will serve as well. First arrange fifteen matches in three rows of four, five, and six respectively. You now take it in traditional turns to remove one or more matches from any single row or all the matches in any single row. As already explained, whoever is left with only one match to take when it is his turn to play loses the game.

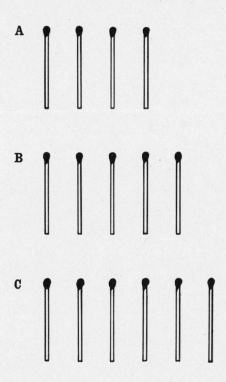

The strategy you have to follow in order to win every time consists of two parts. First, if you open the game, remove either 1 match from Row A, 3 matches from B, or 5 from C. Secondly, when you play again or when you follow your opponent when he plays first, make sure that you leave any one of the following combinations: three rows of matches distributed – in whatever sequence – either 6, 4, 2; 5, 4, 1; 3, 2, 1 or 1, 1, 1; or just two rows with more than one match in a row and the same number in each. A specimen game might go as follows:

1 Your opponent removes two matches from A.
2 You then remove one match from B, leaving 6 in C, 4 in B, 2 in A.
3 He removes 4 matches from C.

4 You then remove all 4 left at B, leaving two rows equal but with more than one match in each row.
5 He can now either take one match from A or C, or both from A or C.
6 If the former, you take the pair that remains and he is left with the last match; if the latter, you take one from the remaining pair, still leaving the last match.

The more you play, the more familiar you will become with the various endings to the game. Play rationally and you should have no problems. Finally, here is one other specimen sequence:

1 You remove one match from A.
2 Your opponent removes 3 matches from B.
3 You remove 5 matches from C, leaving the combination 3, 2, 1.
4 Your opponent removes 1 match from B.
5 You remove 2 from A, leaving 1, 1, 1.
6 He takes one from A.
7 You take one from B.

Once again he has to take the last match. You could almost say "the last straw".

Rattlesneak

On being burgled: "Would you believe it that the rattlesnake to show his appreciation for my hospitality sunk his fangs into the calf of the burglar's leg, stuck his tail out through the flap of the tent and held the intruder fast while he rattled for a policeman."

With little call for dexterity of any kind you can craftily duplicate the classic effects of the three card trick and the three shell game (both to be described later in this book), if you have three small pill boxes that all look the same and a single pill. You place the pill in one of the boxes, then snap all three boxes shut. Moving them around on the table, you defy the sucker to point to the box which he thinks contains the pill. Of course, he never suceeds, a fact made possible by another pill in another pill box held secretly against your wrist by your watch strap or an elastic band.

In explaining the game to the victim, first rattle the pill which he knows about in its box to prove it is there. Make sure, however, that you shake it with your ungimmicked hand. Then, in moving the boxes around, aim at confusing him to the point where he has no alternative but to make a guess at the correct box. If he chooses one of the two empty boxes, pick up the right one and shake it normally. If he points to the box that does hold the pill, pick up instead one of the empty boxes and shake it with the gaffed wrist. He will hear a pill rattling inside a box, but he won't realise that the pill he hears is not the original pill. Your spiel is always the same, "No, *this* one rattles, the other two don't." You can repeat this as often as you wish, as long as you can keep track of the noisy box yourself and don't get your hands confused. Always attempt, however, to finish the sequence when the sucker is legitimately wrong, so that having redirected his attention to the box he should have chosen, he can shake it and, for that matter, take the pill out of the box himself.

If you do not have three similar pill boxes ready to hand, you can achieve the same effect with small match boxes, two empty, one half-full, with a fourth half-full box attached to the wrist. Whatever you use, beware you do not give the game away when you look for the time.

Monte

"Long live the King, but look at the Queen!"

"A little game from Hanky Poo, the black for me, the red for you – all you really have to do is keep your eye on the lady – ten gets you twenty, twenty gets you forty – here we go – keep your eye on the lady." So went the doggerel with which the old-time operators of possibly the most famous swindle of them all commenced their pitch. Today Dai Vernon, the most perfect performer of pure sleight-of-hand in the world, commences his own demonstration with a similar jingle. The Professor, as he is known affectionately to other magicians, has subtly embellished the basic premise of the original game to a point where any of the subterfuges so gained would have made the eyes of the average nineteenth-century Mississippi river boat gambler pop in incredulity. It cannot be the purpose of this book, however, to delve explicitly into what represent the inner secrets of legerdemain as distinct from the dubious wiles of the confidence trickster. More relevant to this volume is an explanation of the basic move on which the standard game, as it is still perpetrated on the streets of London and Manhattan, is based.

The best cards to use are a red queen and two similar black spot cards, say the seven of clubs and the eight of spades. To make them easier to lift from your working surface bend the cards slightly along their length, crimping them – to use the technical term – as shown in the illustration.

With the faces concave, there should be no problem in picking up the face-down cards by their ends. When you bend the cards, place them together so that all will be crimped in the same way.

The key move referred to above and known as "the throw", enables you to pick up two cards in one hand, one of them the queen, then to throw them slowly with their backs face-down on to the table. All seems fair, but as you supposedly throw down the queen, you actually substitute a spot card. Here's how. Place the three crimped cards in a face-down row on the table. You need to known the position of the queen. Now between the pad of the right thumb

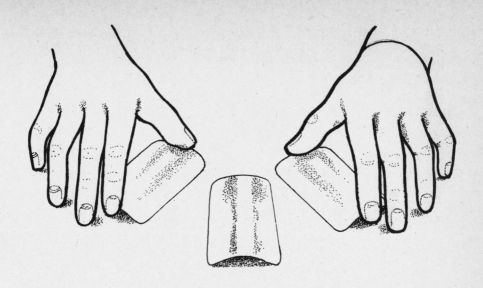

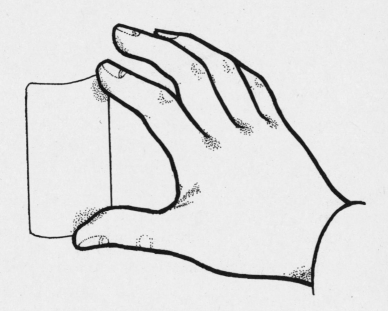

and the tip of the right index finger pick up one of the spot cards by the ends close to the top and bottom right corners. The illustration shows your view at this point.

Raise your hand to show the face to the onlookers. Next pick up the other spot card in a similar fashion in the left hand, again showing its face. Then finally bring your right hand over the queen which you pick up between the tips of the thumb and second finger beneath the first card as shown.

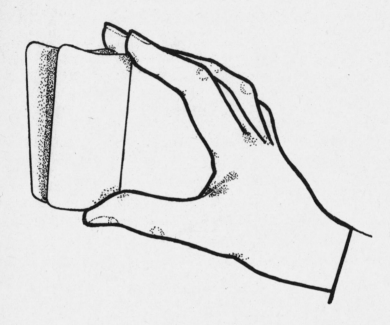

Lift and show the queen to be the bottom card. The hands should be about six to nine inches above the table. In turning the right hand back towards the surface you now appear to throw down the bottom face-down card. What actually happens – with one smooth continuous movement – is that you release the top spot card from between the thumb and index finger and then shift the index finger hold to the queen, at the same time as you release the second finger from the queen. The smaller movement of the fingers is totally hidden by the larger downward sweep of the hand. The spectators now assume that the card on the table is the queen. When they have registered that fact, drop the spot card in the left hand down beside it and finally the remaining "spot" card – in fact, the queen – from your right hand. All this should be done in one easy rhythmic sequence.

Slowly mix the cards around on the table and then offer to pay odds of two to one if the player can find the lady. If you had not allowed the faces of the cards to be seen, the game would be two to one in *your* favour; but since you place the odds in favour of the victim who hopefully has been keeping his eyes open anyhow, logic should dictate to him that he has by far the greater chance of winning. Master the throw, however, and he seldom will. In revealing the sucker's mistake, again pick up the cards as described and you will be all set to play again.

It is advisable to ring the changes on the positions where you throw down the cards and the combinations of moves you make in shifting the cards around on the table prior to inviting the victim to tell you the position of the queen. Always remember to go through the moves and throw legitimately – actually releasing the queen first – at least once before you start accepting bets. The more in fact you study the legitimate movement, so you will gain a clearer indication of the effect the false throw should simulate.

The above move formed the pivot of the routine practised by the most notorious of all monte operators, a character known in sporting circles as "Canada Bill" Jones. Those close to him became so suspicious of the various appearances which he would assume for the world that on the occasion of his funeral, as the coffin was being lowered into the grave, one of the crowd was heard to bet one thousand dollars to five hundred that he was not in the box. That the bystander found no takers is testimony to the longstanding reputation Jones had gained for squeezing through even tighter holes. It was "Canada Bill" who once put into a nutshell the philosophy of his profession: "Suckers have no business with money, anyway." Both the exit and the sentiment are the kind of which Fields would have religiously approved.

Monte-plus

W.C.:   *Did you get your man?*
Officer: *Well, not yet, but I got my woman.*
W.C.:   *Well, that's something.*

As in the classic three card monte sequence, the success of this swindle depends upon an optical illusion. But, while the object is still to "find the lady", this time no digital dexterity is involved.

In addition to five cards, one of which is a queen, you will need a bulldog clip about two inches in length and an ordinary spring clothes peg. Overlap the cards in a straight row with the queen in the centre. Trap the cards within the bulldog clip as shown.

Stress the position of the queen, then holding the clip turn all the cards over. Ask someone to point to the queen and to mark it by fastening the peg over its end. The cards should then look like this:

112

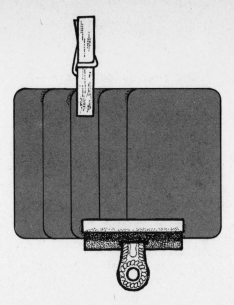

Now turn the cards face-up again and you will be unable to believe your eyes. The peg will never appear to be where it should be, namely on the queen, only on the end card.

The whole ruse depends upon the discrepancy between the ways in which cards overlap when they are face-up and when they are face-down. Make sure that the peg is not too tight so that the sucker can handle it easily, trapping the several layers of card with no problem.

Garter

"The only way I work is cash on the barrel-head!"

In this updated version of the ancient swindle, "Pricking the Garter", a permanent fixture of dock-fronts long ago when the hustlers would use barrel-heads for their working surface, you appear to offer the sucker a fifty-fifty chance of winning. In actual fact, whether he wins or loses is completely under your control. In olden times the operator would use a soft pliable leather thong – hence the title – about four feet in length. You can as easily use a similar length of string or soft rope.

Holding the two ends of the rope together in your left hand and the centre in your right, twirl the latter inwards and lay the rope on the table in this position:

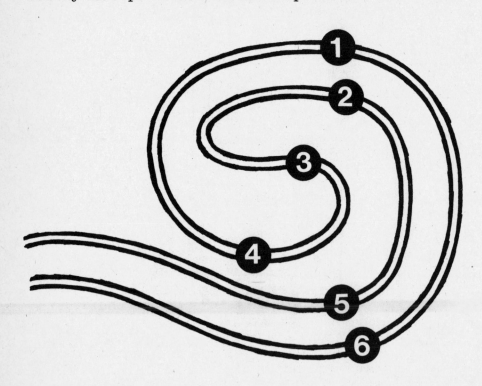

Now pull strand 4 down until it rests alongside 6 and lift 5 alongside 3. This will produce two loops, A and B, in the rope. The result should look as follows:

114

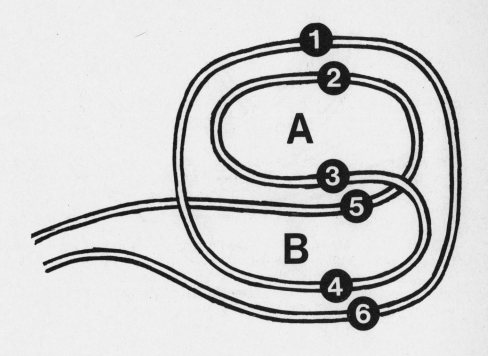

The sucker now has to choose whether to insert his index finger in the centre of either A or B, whereupon the operator will pull at the two ends of the rope. If he puts his finger into the one loop, the rope will come away free. If he inserts it into the other – the correct one – his finger will be caught in the rope when you pull. In order to win, the sucker must trap his finger in such a fashion.

The winning loop is B, a fact that will soon register with the sucker after a few tries. However, at the moment when he thinks he is beginning to grasp the gist of the game, you resort to some subtle hanky-panky. Once again, lay the rope out as in the first illustration, but this time, and without any tell-tale pause, casually put a twist in the final inward twirl as you do so:

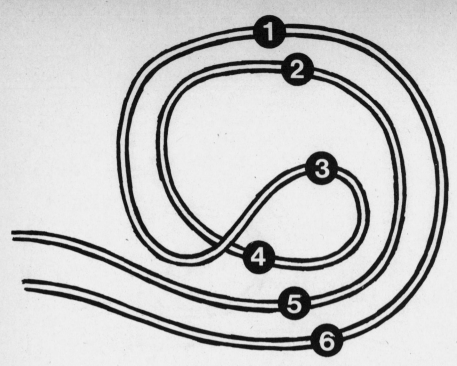

Once again, strand 4 is pulled down to 6 and strand 5 is pushed up to 3. To the most hawk-like pair of eyes there will appear to be no difference in the lay-out, and yet *whichever* loop the sucker attempts to catch with his finger will now come away free when you pull.

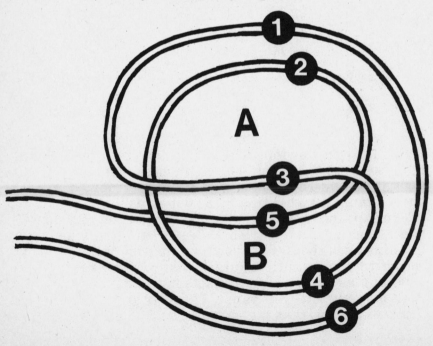

Happily, once the rope has been pulled, all the evidence will have evaporated into thin air! Even if you form the correct lay-out some of the time, the odds will still be in your favour (3 to 1, in fact, if you use it as much as half the time). Whenever he places his finger in the free loop you will have an opportunity to lift a strand or two carefully to show he has lost, replace and then demonstrate with your own index finger trapped in the other loop how he could have won.

The Old Army Game

"A little fun, just now and then,
Is relished by the best of men.
If you have nerve, you may have plenty;
Five draws you ten, and ten draws twenty.
Attention giv'n, I'll show to you,
How Umbrella hides the peek-a-boo.
Select your shell, the one you choose;
If right, you win, if not, you lose;
The game itself is lots of fun;
Jim's chances, though, are two to one;
And I tell you your chance is slim
To win a prize from 'Umbrella Jim'."

The Old Army Game

"Who will be the next to outwit me? A little game of chance. Come one and come all. The old Army Game. This is not a game of chance. It is a game of science and skill." Then, on seeing the mayor approach: "Gambling, my dear friends is the root of all evil. For years I was a victim of this awful scourge, gambling, a helpless pawn in the toils of Beelzebub. Beelzebub – Lucifer."

With the doggerel reproduced on the preceding page, "Jim" Miner, alias the "Umbrella Man", one of the most notorious operators of the three shell game in nineteenth-century America, would begin his spiel. It was Fields, however, who really made this swindle his own. He regarded it with such affection that it became a recurring motif in his films – to the extent that one movie which had no connection whatsoever with the swindle was named after it.

The props you require are three half-walnut shells, a pea, and a suitable working surface. For the latter use a felt cloth, a few thicknesses of newspaper, or a rug. The pea, not a real one, should be about 3/10 of an inch in diameter and fashioned from a piece of fine mesh sponge rubber. The amount of "give" provided by the combination of working surface and pea is what makes the swindle possible. For the shells, carefully slice some nuts into halves with a sharp knife. Choose three halves which look approximately the same, scoop out what remains of the kernel, and then with sandpaper smooth down the inside, getting rid of any jagged edges which might impede the movement of the pea.

You also have to learn one basic move. Place the pea on the surface and cover it with a shell held exactly as in the illustration. Now move the shell forward without lifting it from the surface. You will find after a while that you will acquire the knack whereby the pea will travel out of its own accord into your fingers, where it can be grasped secretly between the pads of the thumb and the second finger. The first illustration shows the move forward, the second shows the position of the pea on reaching its destination, as it would appear to someone looking up beneath your hand – if he could see through the table.

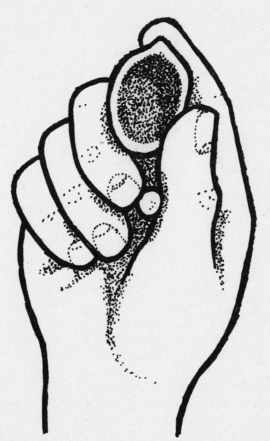

121

Move the shell back and the pea will automatically ride back beneath its cover. Try it a few times and you will find that the pea and the surface do most of the work for you. Because of the give that exists between them, the shell will not appear to lift at all as the pea leaves.

Once you have mastered the move itself, practise pushing a shell forward, leaving it there, moving your hand – now secretly holding the pea – to another shell and drawing that shell back as the pea rides beneath it. This device enables you to control the exact position of the pea at any moment in the game as you move the shells around. Many combinations are possible in actual performance. Here is a suggested sequence. For clarity in understanding the moves imagine the area on which you'll perform as a rectangular grid divided into 6 squares so:

A	B	C
D	E	F

You start with the shells at D, E and F with the pea in front of E.

1 Cover the pea with shell E and move forward, stealing the pea, to A. Move D to B. Move F to C. Draw A back to E, loading the pea. Draw B back to D. Draw C back to F. Ask the sucker to point to the pea. Nothing in fact has happened so far because the pea, under E, is where it should be. Show the pea at E and tell him how easy it is. He must agree.

2 Again cover the pea with E. Move E to B, stealing the pea. Move D to A and F to C. Draw A back to E, loading the pea, B to D, and C to F. He'll point to D whereupon you show the pea back at E.

3 Once again, cover the pea with E. Move E to A, stealing the pea, F to B, D to C. Draw A back to E, C to F, loading the pea, and B to D. This time he'll point to E and you show him the pea at F.

4 Cover the pea with F. Move F to B, stealing the pea, E to A, and D to C. Draw A back to D, loading the pea, B to F and C to E. He'll point to F and you show the pea at D.

5 Cover the pea with D, move forward to A, stealing the pea. move E to B and F to C. Draw A back to E, B to F, loading the pea, and C to D. He'll point to E. You lift F.

In time you'll develop your own combinations to the point where the movement of the shells will become second nature. As a climax, however, ask the sucker to point to one of the shells. Cover the pea with this shell and ask him then to press his forefinger down on the shell. With his finger in position you push the shell slightly closer to him, but in doing so automatically steal away the pea. You don't do anything differently. Just pretend his finger isn't there. Strangely, he won't feel the pea leave and will swear it is still under his finger. Draw back the other two shells, loading the pea under the one nearer you. Take his bet, then watch his expression when you show him the pea under *your* shell and he lifts his finger to check under his.

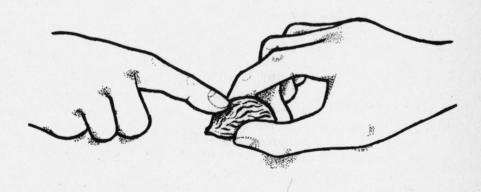

Man:　*You cheated us.*

W.C.:　*Sir, you impugn my honour. My dear old grandfather said, just before they sprung the trap, you can't cheat an honest man. Never give a sucker an even break or smarten up a chump.*

Appendix

Upon standing for the Presidency:
  "When I am elected chief executive of this fair land, amidst thunderous cheering and shouting and throwing of babies out the window, I shall, my fellow citizens, offer no such empty panaceas as a New Deal, or an Old Deal, or even a Re-Deal. No, my friends, the reliable old False Shuffle was good enough for my father and it's good enough for me."

Various items with playing cards have specified the need for false shuffles and false cuts. For complete details the dedicated student should refer either to Scarne or to the classic, *The Expert at the Card Table* by S. W. Erdnase. The following details are merely meant to bridge a technical gap until those books can be consulted.

False shuffle (i): This enables you to keep the order of the entire pack or of an entire packet of cards intact while seemingly mixing them in the sloppiest and therefore the most disarming fashion. Hold the pack face downwards in the left hand. With the left thumb push a few, i.e. about four or five, cards from the top of the pack into the waiting right hand. Now adjust the grip of your left hand and push a few cards this time from the bottom of the pack and receive them on top of those in the right hand. Next push a few cards from the top of the left hand *under* the cards in the right and continue in this fashion, alternating between cards from top and bottom. Remember that the cards that go on top of the right hand cards always come from the bottom of the left hand cards, and that, vice versa, those that go to the bottom of the right hand packet come from the top of the left hand cards. Continue doing this until the left hand cards are exhausted. Repeat the "shuffle" if you wish. The actual effect this has on the cards is that of cutting the pack a number of times. In other words, the essential sequence is not disturbed and it is only necessary to cut the cards at the original top card to bring them back to their original order. The latter may be done openly by fanning the cards with the faces towards you under the pretence of removing the joker or more stealthily by making the top card a key card, a process explained in 'Aces'.

False shuffle (ii): This shuffle enables you to keep one card on top of a pack or packet, while apparently mixing the pack. It should cause you no problem at all if you can do a normal overhand shuffle. Holding the cards in the usual position in the right hand, merely thumb off the top card by itself into the left and then briskly shuffle off all the other cards on top of it. Now take all the cards back into the right hand and shuffle again. Don't worry about the first card this time. It is only necessary to exercise caution as you come to the end of the cards, the last of which should be thumbed singly – back to its starting position.

False cut: This again returns the whole pack to its original sequence. Holding the pack in the right hand from above, fingers at the outer narrow end, thumb at inner, drop about a third of them on the table mentally numbering the pile 1. Drop another similar packet to the right of the pile on the table, numbering this 2. Finally place the rest of the cards to the left of 1, numbering this 3. Now without pausing pick up 2 and place onto 1, and then place 3 onto the pile consisting of 1 and 2. It all seems so disarmingly fair, but the order of the cards has not been disturbed at all. You can vary the ending by picking up 1 and placing it in the left hand, then placing 2 on top, and finally 3 on top of them both. The more you ring this sort of change, the less likely it is that you will be caught.

Acknowledgments

The origins of most of the swindles contained in this book are lost in antiquity. It is sometimes possible, however, to pinpoint an idea to a specific person. With that in mind, I should like to place on record my gratitude to the minds responsible for the following wiles.

Of the items with playing cards, Monte-plus was, I believe, a brainchild of the Canadian comedy conjurer, Joe Stuthard. Kentucky is an adaptation of "Tony Koynini's Derby", a "Magic Wand" publication of George Armstrong from 1952. Likewise Milady can claim kinship with "Strangers from Two Worlds", a mathematical effect described by Stewart James in the magical magazine *Tops* in April 1963. Those interested will find the basic principles used in Second-deal elaborated upon by Harry Lorayne in his book *Close-Up Card Magic*. Look for "Little Fella – Big Fella".

The variation on the classic belt or garter swindle described under Garter was the inspiration of L. Vosburgh Lyons, contributed by him to the 23 July 1943 edition of *The Phoenix*, a prominent magic magazine of that period. Stuart Robson described Inferno, a twist on an old bar game, in the 25 December 1942 issue of the same sheet. Those thwarted in their attempts to "follow the leader" with Twister have the brilliant English magician Alex Elmsley to thank for their frustration. His idea was first published in the 8 January 1955 issue of *Abracadabra*, the world's only magical weekly, which happily – unlike *The Phoenix* – still thrives.

For the introduction to Cocktail, that rarity – an original match puzzle, I am grateful to the delightful *The Pillow-Book Puzzles* by Ivan Morris. The game Matrix was invented by G. W. Lewthwaite and first seen by myself in Martin Gardner's column of "Mathematical Games" in the June 1975 edition of *Scientific American*. Similarly Matrimony is based on the Blades of Grass Game described by the same author in his *Sixth Book of Mathematical Games*.

Anyone seeking more comprehensive information in the fascinating area of probability and proposition bets should consult the excellent quartet of books on gambling by magician Nick Trost or the standard bible on the subject already referred to in these pages, *Scarne's Complete Guide to Gambling*. It was the second volume of Trost's quartet that introduced me to the gambling presentation of the little-known mathematical principle described under Shill. It was Scarne who was the first man to the best of my knowledge who attempted to tear cellophane in print, yet again in *The Phoenix*, 27 November 1942. May that be the only swindle in these pages that *your* sucker ever sees through—literally!

I should also like to thank Darien House Inc. for permission to use the Hirschfeld drawing on page 12. Every effort has been made to trace the copyright holders of quoted material. Should there be any omissions in this respect, I apologise and shall be pleased to make the appropriate acknowledgment in future editions.

Finally my affectionate thanks to those magicians who first introduced me to the delights of deceiving for pleasure and the camaraderie of the magic world. They include Martin Neary— my maternal grandfather, Wizard Edward Beal, Professor Harry Woodley, and Dr. Denis Yetman. I shall be grateful to them always.

About the Author

Born in England in 1945 and educated in classics at Oxford, John Fisher is currently working in an editorial capacity on television production for the BBC. Also an accomplished magician, he is a member of both the Magic Circle and the International Brotherhood of Magicians, and is a regular performer of magic shows on British television.

Among his other books are *John Fisher's Magic Book; The Magic of Lewis and Carroll,* which explores Carroll's interest in conjuring as it relates to his literary work; and *Call Them Irreplaceable,* an appraisal of the style of star quality in the great solo entertainers of the mid-twentieth century.